This invaluable book is an essential addition to offers the reader profound psychological insight into the relationship between grief and memories. Each chapter closes with thoughtful reflective questions reminding the reader that we don't ever get over grief but that we can learn to live alongside it in healing, hopeful, and creative ways.

—**CLAIRE B. WILLIS, LICSW, MA,** CLINICAL SOCIAL WORKER,
AND COAUTHOR OF *OPENING TO GRIEF: FINDING YOUR WAY
FROM LOSS TO PEACE*

Dr. Lamia, a gifted psychologist and educator, has written a deeply personal and empathic book, which pulls together the scientific literature on grief. Readers of this book will find solace and help with integrating their own experiences of personal loss.

—**MARDI HOROWITZ, MD,** DISTINGUISHED PROFESSOR OF PSYCHIATRY,
UNIVERSITY OF CALIFORNIA SAN FRANCISCO, SAN FRANCISCO, CA,
AND AUTHOR OF *GRIEVING AS WELL AS POSSIBLE: AN INSIGHTFUL
GUIDE TO ENCOURAGE GRIEF'S FLOW, NAVIGATE DIFFICULT MOMENTS,
AND PUT YOUR LIFE OR A FRIEND'S LIFE BACK TOGETHER*

Dr. Lamia explains why grief is an ongoing and necessary force in the human mind, and how it is connected to emotion, identity, thoughts, and physiological responses. With a perceptive, humane perspective on the subtleties of life and death, she uses examples from her own life, professional work, and the research literature to address major questions about the role of grief in determining who we are and who we become. Lamia shows how over time and with work, in our grieving moments, we can learn to adapt to major loss, and live with loss. We don't get over major loss. We can and must live with it.

—**JOHN H. HARVEY, PHD,** PROFESSOR EMERITUS, UNIVERSITY OF IOWA,
IOWA CITY, IA, AND FOUNDING AND CONTINUING EDITOR,
JOURNAL OF LOSS AND TRAUMA

Joan Didion let us know grief makes us crazy. Dr. Lamia's book makes sense of the crazy. We expect grief but are reminded we are never prepared. For clinicians and those grieving, reading *Grief Isn't Something to Get Over* clarifies a way to understand and reassemble the fragments of time, emotion, and memory through Dr. Lamia's case narratives, and most profoundly through her own intimate and poignant story.

—**JOAN DRISCOLL, PHD,** CLINICAL PSYCHOLOGIST, KENTFIELD, CA

There is so much confusion about grief in what I call our "grief-impaired culture," and thankfully, Mary Lamia's clear-eyed approach clears up that confusion and helps us reduce unnecessary suffering. In this lyrical book that melds stories of grief (including her own) with the most recent research, she helps us see how crucial memory is to grief, and how the idea of stages of grief, or "getting over" grief is not only wrong, but impossible. Instead, she helps us see that our work in grief is to *adapt* to loss rather than try to avoid or redeem it, and to bring memories of our dearly departed into a new future made possible by their lives, our loss, and our love.

—KARLA McLAREN, MED, AUTHOR OF *THE LANGUAGE OF EMOTIONS: WHAT YOUR FEELINGS ARE TRYING TO TELL YOU* AND *EMBRACING ANXIETY: HOW TO ACCESS THE GENIUS OF THIS VITAL EMOTION*

In *Grief Isn't Something to Get Over*, Mary Lamia tells a very personal story and offers a very professional study on how we deal with the loss of those we love. Confiding in us about dealing as a child with the death of her mother, as an adolescent with the death of her father, and as an adult with the death of her husband, we learn through research and personal experience that the pain and grief sometimes last a lifetime. "Moving on" from grief may be a wish, but it is not a reality. Dr. Lamia details the ways we may cope and perhaps benefit from dealing with the pain and loss we suffer from the death of someone who has been close to us.

—LAWRENCE B. LURIE, MD, DFAPA, CLINICAL PROFESSOR OF PSYCHIATRY, UNIVERSITY OF CALIFORNIA SAN FRANCISCO, SAN FRANCISCO, CA

Dr. Lamia deftly interweaves grief theories and research with her own past and, sadly, her recent experience with loss. The result is a book both highly informative and emotionally moving. I highly recommend this book to anyone seeking to provide help to others or themselves coping with the loss of a loved one.

—MARILYN J. KRIEGER, PHD, COAUTHOR OF *THE WHITE KNIGHT SYNDROME: RESCUING YOURSELF FROM YOUR NEED TO RESCUE OTHERS*

This scholarly meditation on heartbreak belongs in the libraries of therapists, counselors, coaches, clergy, teachers, students, and mourners trying to understand their own grief. In accessible writing replete with personal stories, Mary Lamia explores the emotional, cognitive, and sensory aspects of excruciating loss and shows why well-intentioned pressures to "get over it," "move on," or "find closure" both misunderstand the nature of grief and impede creative adaptations to it. A brilliant and moving book.

—**NANCY McWILLIAMS, PHD, ABPP,** VISITING FULL PROFESSOR, RUTGERS GRADUATE SCHOOL OF APPLIED AND PROFESSIONAL PSYCHOLOGY, PISCATAWAY, NJ

With her characteristic keen intellect and extraordinary empathy, Dr. Mary Lamia brings new understanding and light to a topic too long verboten and shrouded in notions of how those who grieve are supposed to overcome or vanquish emotions of bereavement. This is a clear-sighted and important book by one of our nation's leading psychologists, who makes us see fully how such emotions are not easily dispensed with or compartmentalized and what can be done to allay the pain of grief.

—**MICHAEL KRASNY, PHD,** PROFESSOR EMERITUS OF ENGLISH, SAN FRANCISCO STATE UNIVERSITY, SAN FRANCISCO, CA; AUTHOR; RETIRED HOST OF KQED'S *FORUM*

Mary Lamia is a wise and deeply compassionate guide through the mysteries of loss, memory, and grief. Combining scientific expertise, therapeutic skill, and her own life experience, she has written an invaluable book that will serve as a vital resource for individuals confronting lingering memories of their loved ones and for the professionals who seek to support them through their grief.

—**JEFFERSON A. SINGER, PHD,** FAULK FOUNDATION PROFESSOR OF PSYCHOLOGY, CONNECTICUT COLLEGE, NEW LONDON, CT

In this warmly readable book, Dr. Lamia radically overturns the notion that grief is something you simply process and get over; instead, she asserts, we use memory, in all its many manifestations, to come to terms with and live with it. *Grief Isn't Something to Get Over* is rich with deep knowledge and poignant detail from Lamia's work as a therapist, her own very personal encounters with loss and grief, her delightful common sense, and her thorough analysis of current professional and scientific thinking on the subject. A must-read and a great comfort for anyone who has suffered personal loss, which is, really, all of us.

—**MIRIAM REAL, PHD,** EDUCATOR, ORAL HISTORIAN, MILL VALLEY, CA

With warmth, empathy, and intelligence, Mary Lamia looks at memory in the grief process from a unique perspective. Generously sharing her own experiences with significant loss, as well as examples from patients and friends, she guides us to make sense of the painful process of mourning after a loved one dies. Lamia creates a wonderful metaphor of finding a home for memories of a loved one—which coexist with hope and new meaning from relationships, beauty, and the energy of life.

—DEBORAH COSTELLO, BA, WRITER, EDUCATIONAL TECHNOLOGY CONSULTANT, BURLINGTON, VT

"Get over it!" I'd tell myself. I felt ridiculous for feeling grief as an adult. I couldn't understand how happy events, rites of passage like birthdays, graduations, weddings, etc., caused me anxiety and sadness. I didn't get it, until I read Dr. Lamia's book. My anxiety around birthdays had everything to do with my father's early death, and as Lamia explains throughout the book, the brain keeps our memories as reminders, whether we are aware of them or not. Lamia's explanation of how memories impact grief for years to come, along with her own story of early and recent loss, helped me connect the dots in my own life. Knowing now that it's my memory that's triggering these feelings intellectualizes it for me and makes me more prepared and understanding of the process. Now I can stop telling myself to "get over it!"

—MARA MENACHEM, COMMUNITY ACTIVIST, FASHION WRITER, AND DESIGNER, MARIN COUNTY, CA

Both intensely personal and profoundly universal, Dr. Lamia's book will resonate with all of us who have struggled with overwhelming loss. As a master clinician offering both science and rich experience, she argues that loss, like trauma, is not necessarily redeemable in the way we may hope. Yet this magnificently honest, very human book shows that there is still a path in grief that leads to healing.

—WILLIAM McCOWN, PHD, DIRECTOR, SCHOOL OF BEHAVIOR AND SOCIAL SCIENCES, UNIVERSITY OF LOUISIANA AT MONROE, MONROE, LA

Dr. Mary Lamia's insightful and perceptive book reaches deep into our souls. Her ideas and concepts provide another way of looking at grief beyond the standard Kubler-Ross stage theory. By acknowledging our memories of our lost parent, child, sibling, friends, and more, we are enabled to intertwine the memories of them into our lives in a helpful ongoing and healing manner. Having lost my mother during grad school, I found many parts of this book that directly speak to me. I highly recommend this thought-provoking book into the process of grief.

—JOAN STEIDINGER, PHD, DEPARTMENT OF KINESIOLOGY, SAN JOSE STATE UNIVERSITY, SAN JOSE, CA

Anyone who has suffered the loss of a loved one through death, divorce, or otherwise should read this book. Dr. Lamia, by allowing us insight into her own losses, explains how loss can bring new meaning and new hope into one's life. This book is a tool to learn how to embrace pain and loss and how to adapt to it, rather than get over it. I was sobbing with happiness with the memories of my losses by the time I finished the book. A must-read.

—CHARLOTTE H. HUGGINS, CERTIFIED FAMILY LAW SPECIALIST, MARIN AND SONOMA, CA

Grief is a silent bond with your loved one steeped in poignant memories, a celebration of what was and what could have been. Through vivid personal memories and colorful stories, Dr. Lamia shows us how grief is the sustenance of growth. For me, as a recent widow, this book was a true awakening and a superb tool for healing.

—ISOBEL WIENER, RN, FORMER PSYCHIATRIC NURSE, SAN ANSELMO, CA

GRIEF
isn't something to get over

GRIEF
isn't something to get over

Finding a home for memories and emotions after losing a loved one

MARY LAMIA, *PhD*

 AMERICAN PSYCHOLOGICAL ASSOCIATION

Published by
APA LifeTools
750 First Street, NE
Washington, DC 20002
https://www.apa.org

Order Department
https://www.apa.org/pubs/books
order@apa.org

In the U.K., Europe, Africa, and the Middle East, copies may be ordered from Eurospan
https://www.eurospanbookstore.com/apa
info@eurospangroup.com

Typeset in Sabon by Circle Graphics, Inc., Reisterstown, MD

Printer: Gasch Printing, Odenton, MD
Cover Designer: Mark Karis

Library of Congress Cataloging-in-Publication Data

Names: Lamia, Mary C., author.
Title: Grief isn't something to get over : finding a home for memories and emotions after losing a loved one / by Mary Lamia.
Description: Washington, DC : American Psychological Association, [2022] | Includes bibliographical references.
Identifiers: LCCN 2021044389 (print) | LCCN 2021044390 (ebook) | ISBN 9781433837944 (paperback) | ISBN 9781433837951 (ebook)
Subjects: LCSH: Grief. | Bereavement. | Loss (Psychology)
Classification: LCC BF575.G7 L352 2022 (print) | LCC BF575.G7 (ebook) | DDC 152.4—dc23/eng/20211108
LC record available at https://lccn.loc.gov/2021044389
LC ebook record available at https://lccn.loc.gov/2021044390

https://doi.org/10.1037/0000282-000

Printed in the United States of America

10 9 8 7 6 5 4 3 2 1

For my husband, whose absence, amidst joyful and loving memories of our shared past, evokes the bittersweetness of grief.

CONTENTS

ACKNOWLEDGMENTS

Within the heart of this book are the lived experiences of loss and grief conveyed by friends, acquaintances, clients, students, and anonymous people. Grief is often silently held, so my appreciation is immense that these individuals have shared their responses to loss.

I have tremendous gratitude that Linda McCarter and Tyler Aune believed in me and in my manuscript. The ideas and experiences we exchanged, coupled with the warmth of our interactions, were inspiring. Similarly, Constance Hale and Krissy Jones provided invaluable direction with tremendous heart.

The colleagues, friends, and acquaintances, particularly the many grievers among them who reviewed and endorsed the book, gave me joy with their expressions of interest and high regard for what they learned. I am also inordinately grateful that Marilyn Krieger and William McCown, along with their enduring encouragement of my work, provided light in the darkness of my vulnerability surrounding this book.

The love and support of my cherished family members and friends saw me through the process of completing the manuscript. I realize, and I am sorry, that reading my work may have been challenging and evoked sadness upon becoming aware of my losses and grief.

Beyond the pages of this book, I express loving appreciation to my late husband, Frederick Parris, for "hearing" the silence of grief that I have experienced in my life, which now includes the profound loss of his presence.

GRIEF
isn't something
to get over

CHAPTER I

MEMORIES, EMOTIONS, AND GRIEF

The 20-volume World Book Encyclopedia, *my mother's only extravagant purchase in 1960, became my place to find answers to questions I would have asked her if she hadn't died. My mother could have easily come up with a science presentation topic for a 12-year-old. Instead, I sat on the smooth linoleum floor before the tomes of knowledge, leafing through the unknown. Ultimately, the "M" volume led me to "the mind," inspiring a report on "the unconscious." I did not understand the concept at all. In such situations, I missed my mom, who seemed to know everything and claimed she could fix anything except a broken heart.*

Decades ago, while in training to become a psychologist, I was assigned a client whose profound fear and anguish seemed to lack explanation. He and I eventually linked the recent onset of his symptoms to his age, which was approaching the age his father had been when he died. Dimly aware of the age-matching anniversary, the client had dismissed its importance. His memory, however, did not: It alerted him to the emotions and sensations that had overwhelmed him as a 7-year-old, helplessly watching his father's deterioration and death. Memories of that time had remained quietly within him until he approached age 34, the age of his father when he passed. As we looked back and recognized his grief, his anxiety slowly diminished, and the unbearable depression lifted.

During my work with this man, I silently recalled my own childhood experiences of loss. Inhabiting a dark corner of my mind from the time I was an 11-year-old was a sense that my life, like my mother's, would be over at age 40-something. Logically, and perhaps self-assuredly, I assumed that my awareness of the potential unconscious impact of age-matching anniversaries allowed me to escape my client's emotional struggle. However, conscious knowledge does not eliminate memories that script our present emotional responses and influence how we govern our lives. Every so often, I found myself calculating the years until I would reach the age of my mother's death.

My father, brokenhearted from my mother's passing, did not show me how to deal with death, let alone how to have a happy or long life after such a loss. Professing his wish to be in heaven with my mother, my father died from heart disease 10 years later, surrendering to a religiously acceptable form of suicide by declining vital surgery. I was then a young adult without living parents, and had only memories to keep them present within me.

In countless ways, and to varying degrees, images based on our memories keep us close to loved ones who have died. Yet memories also contain painful reminders of irretrievable joy. Without positive emotional memories and imagery to arouse it, grief is absent. Remembering is what makes us grieve.

Our unique memory system enables us to gather, classify, preserve, and call up a great variety of information from many different sources. Consciously or unconsciously, our memories can reproduce past experiences and simulate present and future possibilities. As such, memory is an essential tool we use for adapting to various circumstances. In situations involving loss, however, new information does not align with our existing memories: Although recent memories inform us of the loved one's absence, more distant memories remind us of their presence. How we reconcile this clashing information influences our responses to loss. In this book, I hope to illuminate how memory interfaces with loss in interesting and unusual ways.

MEMORIES AND GRIEF

We may want to do something to get rid of our grief, but grief is not the true problem. Our suffering results from memories of a loved one that trigger distress or anguish. The experience of grief involves a comparison of the present with the contents of our memories. Recalling enjoyable moments with a departed person—a mother's smile, a father's hug, or a child's laughter—may remind us of what we miss. Memories activated by situations, places, or circumstances—the magic of a holiday, a favorite restaurant, or a trip to the beach—may draw attention to the deceased and the positive emotions we recall sharing with them. A mere gist of a memory, activated by an image, a smell, or a song, can make us aware of feelings and sensations associated with a lost loved one, even without our conscious awareness of why we are experiencing those feelings or sensations at a given moment. Memories of enjoyable moments we once shared with someone who has died are not something we can, or would want to, forget. Given our lifelong ability to remember, grief is not something we just process and get over.

Many attempts to make sense of grief, whether books, blogs, or self-help seminars, have ignored the role of human memory. Consider the concept of a continuing bond with the deceased. If we share a life with someone, we accrue memories of the past, and we store dreams and expectations. We find it difficult to reconcile their death with our anticipated future. In essence, the continuing bond fits into a mental framework or schema that integrates our memories of someone while they were living with our recent memories of their absence and our current experience of life without them. Thus, keeping deceased loved ones with us, in whatever way we may do so, resolves the painful discrepancy between current reality and past memories.

GRIEF AS PERSONAL AND SILENTLY HELD

Grief is uniquely personal. Responses to loss are as distinctive as the individuals who experience them. There may be some generalizable similarities and patterns among people, but there is no template for the grief experience. Our memories and our relationship to the deceased, along with the culture and environment in which we were raised, influence how we respond and adjust to loss.

I have a friend who lost her fiancé in a tragic accident 20 years ago. Her subsequent successful business career and later marriage would lead most of us to assume that her past loss was a distant memory. One day, something about the conversation we were having on a walk together enabled me to ask how the loss affected her now. She responded,

> When he died, it left a permanent imprint on my soul. I think about him every day and know that someday I will be with him. Sometimes I think to myself that at least I knew what that kind of love was. But there are times when I still grieve for what should have been, or could have been.

The perception that a person has "moved on" from the loss of a loved one may have little to do with what they feel inside. Many of us continue to hold silent bonds with the deceased. The bereaved, while appearing otherwise as perfectly happy people, may compartmentalize their thoughts and feelings around a loss. In collusion with friends, relatives, therapists, and researchers who may not inquire, this silence among grievers is part of our elusive understanding of grief. We may generally ask how someone is doing after a loss but, once they appear to have resumed day-to-day life, we forget to ask, or we do not probe. Some mourners may keep bonds with deceased loved ones to themselves, considering a connection with someone who has died as sacred, personal, or even shameful. Is it bad manners to bring up the deceased, given that it may impose the pain or shame of loss on the survivor, or are we sparing ourselves by not asking? In this regard, one of my grieving clients once said, "People don't ask questions, but they also don't want to know the answers." This ignorance-is-bliss reflex also prevents us from understanding grief.

ACCEPTANCE AND CLOSURE DO NOT APPLY TO LOSS

People who mourn may want to get over their immediate emotional distress, but they do not necessarily want to forget the person who has died. The misguided but common notion that grief is time limited leads many people to believe that in order to achieve some kind of closure they must relinquish attachments. But closure requires resolution. Thoughts, situations, places, or circumstances activate memories that draw attention to our loss, so we often assume that the attainment of closure arrives at a time when we are impervious to memory. Moreover, many people quietly want to embrace memories of their deceased loved ones. When an acquaintance of mine, Michael, told me that two of his young children had died, he added, "I don't want to lose these memories. Memories are all I have left of them." Instead of "getting over" grief, we can adapt by understanding how memories activate grief and accepting the swirl of emotions we feel. Yet *acceptance*, like *closure*, is another misunderstood concept regarding the bereaved that calls for exploration. The unreality one feels, which often is misconstrued as a lack of acceptance of a loss, often is merely an attempt to align that loss with one's memories. We may fully accept a loved one's absence, but our memory assumes the person is still present.

MANY KINDS OF LOSS CREATE GRIEF

Death is a conspicuous loss. This book focuses on the death of a loved one; however, people carry many kinds of grief-related memories. Grief also attends the loss of an intact family because of divorce, or the mysterious disappearance of a pet, or a parent's descent into dementia, or parents whose children sustain brain damage in an accident, or a sibling who develops a serious mental illness. Sometimes the death of a perpetrator of trauma or violence triggers grief in a victim. Some people experience *collective grief*, such as members of a community whose homes have been destroyed by a wildfire, or the doctors and nurses who coped with the ravages of the COVID-19 pandemic. Sometimes we believe that we are not entitled to grieve less conspicuous losses, or we think that others will judge our grief as illegitimate. We grieve because we remember when things were different.

NARRATIVES AND AUTOBIOGRAPHICAL CONTENT

Grievers tend to convey facts and information about loss, such as when and how someone died, instead of their lived experience of grief and how it has affected them. Throughout this book I include disguised narratives of clients, friends, acquaintances, strangers, and students who have shared with me their emotional memories of grief-related experiences. Other stories are included from anonymous people who have commented on my blog posts or written to me.

In each chapter, including this introductory one, I begin with my own lived experience of loss, and throughout the book I integrate into the discussion many other experiences. During my 4 decades of practice as a psychologist, I would not have imposed my own memories of grief on clients who deserved to have my attention focused entirely on their own lives. In fact, one of the conventions of psychotherapy is for the therapist to remain a blank slate, a mirror for the client. Nevertheless, the personality of the therapist is evident. I am certain none of my clients imagined that my upbeat demeanor emerged from a history of loss, yet the grief I have experienced has contributed to who I am. In this book, I share aspects of my own journey to underscore my point that our memories of people we loved and lost can script who we become. I found that I had more to share than I had anticipated, something I describe at the end of this chapter.

WHAT TO EXPECT

This book's primary purpose is to offer readers psychological insights so they can make sense of the grieving process and more deeply understand the bereavement they are going through. Memories play a significant role in our lives and affect our responses to loss, so how do we understand them? Chapter 2 explores how implicit, explicit, episodic, emotional, and autobiographical memories interface with the experience of loss. We will look at deep emotions as well as everyday issues, such as why some bereaved people have trouble concentrating and often find themselves losing gloves, keys, or a piece of jewelry.

The synthesis of a lifetime of memories creates our sense of self and our identity, yet when our identity is intertwined with a person who dies, our self-definition may be shaken. In Chapter 3, we explore the concepts of self and identity and their relation to self-defining memories, attachment, and prolonged grief. In the face of loss, silent grief may have a special meaning and purpose.

When positive emotional memories commingle with the reality of loss, the outcome may result in bittersweet longing or in the emptiness of depression. Chapter 4 focuses on the myriad emotions related to loss and why some so confuse us. We will look at how emotions work; how various emotions commingle in grief experiences, including trauma; and how present events may trigger memories, including vivid ones. The chapter also delves into misunderstandings of grief. Moreover, we explore how we might experience the progressive physical decline of a loved one as a loss or as a *strain trauma* that may affect one's sense of self, identity, physical health, relationships, and behavior.

The logic of grief is mysterious, as enigmatic as the biographies of people who encounter it. How we think influences our responses to loss, and this is the subject of Chapter 5. Our cognitions— thoughts or imagery—provide meaning to our emotions. Because the deceased still reside within our memories, our ability to imagine them enables us to reconcile the past with the present by continuing our bonds with them. We can project their presence into the external world and, in some cases, make sense of loss and create meaning from it.

In Chapter 6, we explore sensory memories and physiological responses concerning loss. The chapter explains why a particular sensory experience, such as a certain smell or taste, may reawaken images and past events. We look at complex physiological reactions like what is known as "broken heart syndrome," which can accompany grief.

Memory transforms us: We carry the person we lost with us to help inform the present and future. In Chapter 7, we consider how we gain perspective about ourselves and our experiences after a loss. Just as chiaroscuro—the effect of contrasted light and shadow—in painting sharpens our view of a subject, memories that are a shadow of loss heighten our perception of the deceased. The chapter explores how we can assimilate memories of the people we loved and lost to make them shimmer in our present lives. The final chapter, Chapter 8, contains some concluding thoughts.

Diverse opinions, including viewpoints and assumptions about loss and grief, are common in psychological research. Some perspectives regarding how we grieve were presumed valid for decades only to be refuted in the decades that followed. Contemporary researchers continue to grapple with issues surrounding loss, such as whether it is healthier to share our narratives rather than privately hold our grief, or whether finding meaning in loss as opposed to finding meaning in life, is necessarily helpful to grievers. Throughout the chapters, I introduce readers to diverse opinions on many issues concerning grief and how people psychologically engage with loss.

Despite the controversies that exist, my thesis is consistent: Grief isn't something we get over through absorbing a loss, traversing various stages of grief, or moving on in some way. However, we are not doomed to a lifetime of suffering from our losses. Grief has rich meaning. The people we have lost maintain a presence within our emotions, thoughts, imagery, and sensations linked to memories of them that are activated throughout our lives. Whether we encourage or discourage their presence, loved ones who have died are always alive within us.

AN UNEXPECTED ADDITION

As a long holiday weekend approached, I was looking forward to completing suggested edits for the manuscript for this book. Instead, I found myself in a hospital intensive care unit, sitting next to a bed where my husband of 44 years lay unconscious and on life support following a significant stroke. I had found him on the patio, slumped back in a chair, with rasping breaths and a vacant sideways gaze and not responding to my voice. Three days later, my two sons, his sister, and I held our hands over his heart as he took his last breath.

In the following weeks, memories of joyful moments and enjoyable times he and I had shared entered my mind, triggered by the smallest circumstances, such as passing the hardware store where we had bought parts for a challenging plumbing job, or looking at the antique clock and remembering how he would make the cuckoo bird come out to delight our grandson. True to the distress that is grief, my musings centered on mutual enjoyment that, juxtaposed with loss, create painful feelings. I recall the night my husband read the manuscript for this book. Hours later, he came into my study and in a tearful voice told me that, after all these years together, he had learned so many things I had experienced that he hadn't known. Yes, so much of grief is enveloped in the silence of personal memories. Some of those memories, at any given time, may not have words or may seem impossible to convey, even to the people we love. I constantly find myself adjusting my perceptions of the meaning of our shared life to his presence that now exists only as an image within me. Thus, I have revised this book to include my grief upon losing him.

CHAPTER 2

WHY WE REMEMBER

My mother gestured that she wanted me to come close, so I curled up next to her in the bed. "I'm going to go to heaven," she said. The word "No!" spontaneously came out of my mouth, and I began to cry. Then, with calm objectivity, she added, "Take care of your father and brother."

Weeks later, amidst foreboding hospital aromas, I stood at my mother's bedside along with family members. A priest arrived to give her last rites—a collection of Catholic sacraments administered shortly before someone's death. As he began, I was overcome with emotion and started to sob. An aunt shushed me, conveying that my crying was disrespectful to the priest, who was attempting to perform sacred duties. Immediately, I was emotionless, and an unremitting silence remained within me throughout my mother's death and funeral.

> **The experience of grief involves a comparison of the present moment with the contents of our memories.**

Our accumulated memories of the sights, sounds, smells, words, and feelings we have encountered in past situations instantaneously inform everything we experience in the present. A pattern-matching of the present and past is one of the fundamental characteristics of brain functioning. The experience of grief involves a comparison of the present moment with the contents of our memories in several different ways. Painful or traumatic memories and sensations may be recalled when a current experience matches a pattern stored in our minds. For me, hospital smells activate remnants of memories of when I felt unpleasant sensations. However, when something in our present life evokes a pleasurable memory of the deceased, we may perceive the memory not as enjoyable but instead as painful or intrusive. The happy moments we recall may seem bittersweet when flavored by the sadness of loss. At other times, though, we can find comfort in mentally time-traveling into the array of pleasant memories of a loved one who has died and our relationship with that person.

It's not easy to reconcile memories of someone's presence with the fact of their physical absence. Understanding some of the basics of how memory works can provide perspective on why we grieve and how our memory system attempts to make sense of loss in interesting ways.

THE WAYS WE REMEMBER

Memory is not only a means of recollecting and reconstructing the past but also an adaptive process that enables us to use past experiences and information to imagine present and future possibilities (Schacter, 2012). If we were unable to compare immediate experiences with those in our memory, every situation would be novel. We would have to repeatedly relearn everything, from simple tasks to how to deal with perils that await us (Nathanson, 1992). In this way, memories are patterns based on the scenes in our lives; they become stored in our brain's neural network and are later used to inform us.[1] These patterns influence the ways we later respond to similar situations (Addis et al., 2008; Kandel, 1998). Our brain automatically cleans our closet of memories so that new neurons can take the place of old ones; thus, the most significant memories may become stronger while unimportant ones weaken. Therefore, some memories fade, and others seem more pronounced.

Memory is not a single entity but is composed of separate interacting systems and subsystems (Schacter et al., 1993). The renowned cognitive scientist and memory researcher Endel Tulving, intrigued by the abundance of terms that modified the word "memory," found 256 different kinds of memory described by researchers (Tulving, 2007). For our purposes, I describe only some of the primary memory subsystems, those prominent in loss and grief.

Implicit and Explicit Memories

When we tie our shoes, write our names, or ride our bikes, we are unaware of the memories that enable our ability to do so. This kind of memory is referred to as *implicit memory*. Implicit memory affects our present behavior without our conscious awareness. In contrast, *explicit memories* involve consciously recalled factual and autobiographical information. An example of explicit memory is when we consciously recall scenes of learning how to tie our shoes or the patience of the person who taught us.

Implicit memory is fundamental to many of our behaviors, emotions, and mental images, and it occurs without conscious processing or recognition of how past experiences influence our present

---

[1]In a technical sense, memory represents the way the brain encodes experiences through connectivity among neurons and through the activation of neuronal firing patterns (Siegel, 2001).

reality (Siegel, 2010). Implicit memories silently guide our cognitive, emotional, and social judgments, priming us to respond to a present situation on the basis of the accumulation of past implicit memories (Schacter et al., 1993). The far-reaching influence of implicit memories involves our attraction to, or infatuations with, certain people (T. L. Lewis et al., 2000). When activated, an implicit memory registers as a feeling, image, or flashback within us, seemingly from out of nowhere. Because implicit memories are unconscious, they may lead us to wonder, "Why am I thinking about that right now?" or "Why am I drawn to this person?"

> **A heavy mood or intense emotion may result from implicit memories related to loss.**

Implicit memory involves brain regions responsible for emotional, behavioral, and perceptual memories; these create a mental model that enables us to imagine the future (Ingvar, 1985; Siegel, 2010). Quietly working for us and keeping its own calendar, our implicit memory tracks essential dates and places, including anniversaries and markers of significant losses. People are often unaware of markers that may trigger emotional responses, such as passing by a restaurant where you ate with a loved one or the expected birth date of a child lost to miscarriage (McWilliams, 1999). We may instead have a day or week when, for no apparent reason, our mood seems heavy. An implicit memory may account for that mood.

Given the stealthy nature of implicit memories, their occurrence may create moments of intense emotion that seem illogical. As an example, Susan explained that late afternoons weighed on her in the weeks after her husband's death. Sudden intolerable anguish, a flood of tears, or a stomachache would lead her to wonder if she wanted to go on living. When an implicit memory emerges, we are unaware that something from the past is being recalled, even though we may have intrusive feelings, behavioral reactions, perceptions, and bodily sensations (Siegel, 2010). Susan eventually realized these episodes always happened around the time of day she had typically anticipated her husband's arrival home from work. He was always there, exactly on time. When he did not arrive, despite the fact that her memory told her it was time for him to be there, she felt stricken.

Implicit memory constructs mental models from repeated events, making use of our capacity to generalize from experience by encoding our emotions, perceptions, and bodily sensations (Siegel, 2010). The work of our implicit memory primes us, in a sense, to know what to expect. The model in Susan's implicit memory involved her excitement upon hearing her husband's car enter the garage and greeting him with a hug when he walked in. Her inner world was primed to feel and expect something at a specific time.

Implicit memories do not necessarily remain an unconscious enigma. The puzzle pieces of implicit memory may later be put together as explicit memories, thus becoming conscious autobiographical information (Siegel, 2010). This isn't necessarily a relief. For example, Susan later associated the daily ritual of enjoying her husband's return home with her unbearable sadness about his absence. Her way of adjusting to her new reality was to take a walk with a friend that time of day or do enjoyable errands. As weeks passed and the intensity of her grief subsided, she could tolerate the wave of sadness when she was home at the critical hour. On occasion, she imagined her husband coming through the door, and she would excitedly call out, "Hi, Evan!" Then, amused at herself, she would laugh.

As an aside, some bereavement research indicates that resilient people tend not to use coping strategies, such as avoidance or distraction; they don't evade thinking about the loss by deliberately occupying their minds to avoid confronting pain (Bonanno, 2010). Susan, however, realized she needed to face her painful situation after a period in which the pangs of grief had lessened.

> **Grieving people may benefit from an awareness of what they can tolerate at a given moment and can deliberately use coping strategies to avoid their pain.**

Avoidance and distraction have their place in bereavement. Instead of resisting a defensive or coping response (as though it indicates something is wrong with us) in the early weeks or months of grieving, we might benefit from maintaining an awareness of what we can tolerate at a given point in time. In this way, being resilient involves mindfully monitoring emotional responses and taking care of our emotional well-being. Self-care may temporarily require defensive maneuvers. After all, psychological defenses exist for a reason: Sometimes we need them. Friends, family members, and psychotherapists should never attempt to tear down the protection that people have necessarily erected until a firm foothold can be established that will keep them standing. Therefore, if avoidance and distraction help us get through the early period after loss, such as doing something positive that diverts our attention away from what we feel, not to worry: These are perfectly healthy and adaptive coping mechanisms.

Episodic Memory

Intentionally or consciously recalled memories of sensations, emotions, and associations related to significant personal experiences are known as *episodic memories*. They involve clearly remembered key events, such as the first time you met the person who became your long-term partner. When we retrieve an episodic memory, we engage in mental time travel, whereby we are aware of ourselves in the present while recalling ourselves at a particular time in the past or projecting ourselves into an imagined future (Wheeler et al., 1997). Similarly, whenever we wonder what a deceased loved one would feel or think about a present situation, we are using mental time travel to transport their past images into our present circumstances. As a simple example to illustrate, on one recent day I happened to turn on a Giants baseball game, and with every significant play I imagined how my husband would have responded. In a sense, I transported his image into the present as though he were watching along with me.

In general, episodic memories enable us to imagine scenarios that can positively shape the future (Addis et al., 2008). For example, embedded in my memory is a scene in which my father is sitting at a desk, pencil in hand. A small lamp illuminates the well-worn math book that consumes his attention. In my memory, the scene portrays his determination to learn beyond his eighth-grade education, and his efforts inspired me to value learning. This image of his presence, which I have summoned many times throughout my life, seemed to guide me as I worked to accomplish my goals. I think in some way I hoped that, somehow, he would know about every little achievement, even though he was not alive to witness them.

An important subset of episodic memory is *emotional memory*. Chapter 4 is devoted to a discussion of emotional memories and the emotions experienced in grief. For now, let's take a look at another significant subset of episodic memory: autobiographical memory.

Autobiographical Memory

The Greek prefix "auto-," which refers to "self," is part of the word "autobiography," namely, a history of a person that is written by that person. *Autobiographical memory* is the recollection of a sequence of personally significant experiences, each of which represents a clustered set of episodic memories (Siegel, 2010). In essence, autobiographical memory provides knowledge of the self in the past and allows us to project that self into the future (A. Baddeley, 1988; Bluck, 2003). Autobiographical memories enable us to perceive continuity in our lives, direct us in ways that help us solve present problems, and promote our social interaction by providing material for conversations with others (A. Baddeley, 1988; Bluck, 2003).

Like all memory, autobiographical memory protects us by helping us plan or prepare for similar future experiences. It is no mystery, then, why losing a significant person may later lead us to question our own longevity. Similarly, on the basis of the future-warning role of autobiographical memories, children who lose one parent may become concerned about the remaining parent's well-being, and later in their lives they may be overly mindful about the preservation of loved ones, even to the point of obsessing about their health or safety. For example, after my husband's death, one of my sons proposed that I text them every day, just to let them know I am fine. Understanding the anxiety one experiences with losing a parent and worrying about the well-being of the other parent made it easier to comply.

Later in this chapter, I discuss how memories may be distorted. For now, bear in mind that, according to memory researchers, memories of any recollected scene may be quite accurate, or they may be entirely flawed (e.g., Brewin et al., 2020). Some of our memories become distorted on the basis of the enormous amount of information we hold about the past and because interference between memories can occur (Kuhl et al., 2011; McClelland et al., 1995). A typical and mundane error of interference happens, for example, when a memory of where you last placed your car keys competes with earlier such memories (Gallo & Wheeler, 2013). A vague memory may inform where you put them, but an erroneous competing memory, such as where you put the keys 2 days ago, may interfere. In this case, the habit of always putting your keys in the same place may help you avoid frustration.

Recalling memories related to severe illness or death is more complicated than remembering where we put our keys. When a loved one is repeatedly hospitalized, for instance, we may have many competing memories of being at their bedside, the events that took place, and the various emotions we experienced at different times. It is important to know that how we grieve has less to do with the *accuracy* of memories than how we *experience* our memories and what we *do* with them (Bonanno, 2010). This is a significant component of autobiographical memory as it pertains to grief: We do not grieve the facts or exact details of our relationship with someone who has died; instead, our grief is about what we remember of the relationship (Bonanno, 2010).

Accumulated autobiographical memories, along with our future intentions, create a *narrative self*, also known as our *narrative self-definition* (Gallagher, 2000). Broadly defined, our narrative self represents our self-image: a self with a past and a future in the stories we tell about ourselves, what others say about us, and descriptions about our various roles in life (Dennett, 1992). Sociocultural factors, such as gender, class, ethnicity, race, religion, and sexual orientation, are critical to shaping one's narrative self-definition (Singer, 2004). Autobiographical memories based on experiences of grief become part of our narrative self.

In my case, my autobiographical memories led me to plan for a future as a psychologist, imagining that, unlike my mother, I could possibly heal the brokenhearted. There actually is a disorder cardiologists have labeled *broken heart syndrome* (Mayo Clinic Staff, 2020). It results from extremely stressful emotional circumstances, and I say more about it in Chapter 6. My father's cardiac issues resulted from having rheumatic fever as a child; however, be that as it may, nothing could soothe, let alone repair, his metaphorical broken heart after my mother's death. As I studied for my life's work, I put my faith in Sigmund Freud, who had insisted that conveying narratives was reparative. Freud's interest in the work of William Shakespeare may have inspired his belief in what became known as "the talking cure." In Act 4, Scene 3, of *Macbeth*, Shakespeare (1623/2003) wrote:

> Give sorrow words; the grief that does not speak
> Whispers the o'er fraught heart and bids it break.

This belief in the power of words over grief runs deep in Western culture, and, to an extent, it worked for me. Conveying our grief-related narratives to a psychotherapist, grief group, trusted friend, or new acquaintance certainly is relieving for many different reasons, but in particular because the process connects us with others. Even so, in my training as a psychologist and psychoanalyst I was misguided in thinking that catharsis could heal grief, or at least ensure that it would not resurface. Moreover, I was mistaken in not challenging the notion that grief is a process that enables closure. Now, after decades of practice, further study, and life experience, I see that emotional or traumatic experiences reside in our memories, so simply resolving them is not something we do. We can, however, eventually find a home in our mind for our most painful experiences.

Closure is impossible because we cannot erase memories. Eventually, though, we can find a home in our mind for our most painful experiences.

Autobiographical memories activated by a thought, situation, place, or circumstance may repeatedly draw our attention to a loss. Achieving some kind of closure is thus impossible because we cannot erase implicit or explicit memories. Some researchers assert that because memories involve neuronal connections linking them to other memories, thinking or talking about a loss-related memory may actually strengthen traces of its neural pathway (O'Connor & McConnell, 2018). Therefore, we are more likely to remember, rather than to forget. Of course, *not* thinking about significant losses in our lives is impossible. The gradual obscuring of memories regarding the deceased may take years, and even a lifetime, because of the powerful branched memories we hold (O'Connor & McConnell, 2018).

A significant loss alters both the narrative of our lives and the sense of continuity within our autobiographical memories. Although autobiographical memories can help prepare us for what is to come, the sense of discontinuity resulting from loss necessitates that we learn how to revise an anticipated future. Similarly, disruption to our sense of continuity occurs if we lose a job, a home, or a friendship. Practically speaking, remembering is a tool that can be used for learning and adaptation, yet sometimes, especially in the case of traumatic loss, it is challenging to know what the lesson is supposed to be.

Autobiographical Memory and Trauma

Memories of a traumatic loss are part of a particular class of autobiographical memories (Ehlers & Clark, 2000). *Flashbulb memories* occur when a person is informed about a surprising or disturbing moment or encounters a consequential or emotionally arousing event (Brown & Kulik, 1977). These memories have exceptional vividness, illumination, and brevity—like a snapshot of a moment in time

(Brown & Kulik, 1977). Flashbulb memories involve brief perceptual fragments and isolated details of the scene experienced during the event, and they often recur in the form of visual images (Ehlers et al., 2004; Muzzulini et al., 2020). The vivid childhood scene I described at the beginning of this chapter regarding my mother receiving last rites is an example of a flashbulb memory, as is the image of finding my husband suffering from a stroke. Another is the image of one of the planes hitting the World Trade Center towers on September 11, 2001.

A *traumatic memory* is similar in that it involves visually detailed but fragmented qualities. Traumatic experiences may overwhelm our ability to cope with and adjust to events and may call into question the basic assumptions that organize our sense of ourselves and the world (Kauffman, 2002b). Traumatic events that become central in our life story have historically been viewed as part of a maladaptive process that may increase symptoms of posttraumatic stress disorder (PTSD; Broadbridge, 2018). This theoretical perspective proposes that symptoms of PTSD are caused by poor integration of the traumatic event into one's memory, which results in *fragmented recall* (e.g., Brewin, 2016; Horowitz, 1976). In this regard, the intense terror of trauma alters attention mechanisms and, as a result, explicit details of the event are not well remembered (Demos, 2001). Thus, according to this theory, the two memory systems (i.e., explicit and implicit) become disconnected. The explicit recall of the traumatic event is impaired, and there may be few explicit memories, but the somatic, emotional, and behavioral sensations represented in implicit memory can maintain and activate emotions that result in PTSD symptoms.

A more recent model of PTSD challenges the assumption that PTSD symptoms result from a lack of integration. The *autobiographical memory model* suggests that symptoms result from an overly integrated memory of the trauma, which then increases the accessibility of the event in memory (Berntsen & Rubin, 2006; Rubin et al., 2008). Therefore, within autobiographical memory the traumatic memory becomes an anchoring event, which causes the individual to overestimate the occurrence of future negative events (Broadbridge, 2018).

Traumatic losses, such as the accidental death of a child or the loss of a loved one resulting from murder or suicide, leave survivors shocked and helpless, as well as remorseful about what was left unsaid or undone (Tedeschi & Calhoun, 2012). Losing a child or parent to suicide is especially painful, even devastating. Dominant themes in a study of people whose loved ones died by suicide included a lifelong struggle to understand the loss along with a sense of a lack of resolution about the death (O'Neil, 2020).

Although my father's death was a passive suicidal act in that he refused surgery that would have prolonged his life, his circumstances at the time seemed to justify his choice. He wanted to join my mother in heaven, he was unhappy in his marriage to my stepmother, his children had reached adulthood, and his initial heart surgery 8 years earlier had been extraordinarily painful. Because he did not divulge his choice to anyone but his physician, it was only in retrospect and upon gaining that information from his physician that I could make sense of it.

In my work as a psychologist, having witnessed this kind of passive suicide, however, I have wondered what that decision was like for my father. In one instance, a long-term client who had been diagnosed with a progressive cancer decided to reject treatment, asking me to meet with him for as long as possible. As he approached the end of his life, and until the week he died, we agreed to talk by telephone. Knowing this client had suffered a serious romantic heartbreak before his diagnosis led me to recall my father's circumstances and question this client's decision to die. I ultimately honored his decision and was with him as long as possible. Another client, who had a kind and loving spirit, made a similar decision and asked for my help in finding peace about her tumultuous relationship with one of her adult children before she died. On the day of her last visit, she handed me a little music box she had made. Every so often I wind it up and listen to it play. These situations led me to recall, in the case of my father, that I hadn't been given an opportunity to say goodbye. Goodbyes, however, are only a single remembered event in a lifetime.

> **Goodbyes are only a single remembered event in a lifetime.**

For many years I did not consider my father's death a passive suicidal act because, as a child, I had witnessed an actual traumatic suicide. Several months after my mother's death, my father became concerned about our next-door neighbor, whose wife had left him. The man was drinking heavily and threatening suicide. My father took food to the neighbor and encouraged his sobriety. Intentionally leaving on the gas of an unlit stove, then lighting a match, our neighbor set off a fiery explosion that blew out a wall from his home, and him along with it. On our tiny front lawn lay our neighbor in smoldering clothing, screaming, "Help me!" He later died in the hospital. My fear of fire and explosions were heightened for many years afterward. Memory prepares us to anticipate whatever we have already experienced.

Loss of a Child

In my clinical practice, people who have had recent experiences regarding the death of a child endure pain that seems beyond the human capacity to endure. The loss of an unborn child is very painful as well. Although parents have not accumulated memories of the child's life outside the womb, they have memories of their child's imagined life prior to birth. Memories do not necessarily contain actual experiences; they also include imagined ones. For example, during pregnancy the parents may consider the personality of their unborn child based on movements in the womb, wonder who their child is going to be, or speculate about the child's appearance. Considering what to name the child and knowing or imagining their gender creates a reality, including expectancies and imagined scenes. If that child dies, the parents' memories of what they imagined remain and become a part of their grief.

It is interesting that what led Freud to alter his theories related to loss and grieving were his own experiences related to losing a child and a grandchild. Early in his work, Freud misunderstood grief. In 1917, he wrote *Mourning and Melancholia*, in which he theorized that normal mourning is time limited. Freud described a process whereby a mourner repeatedly confronts the reality of the loss, gradually withdrawing psychic energy invested in and attached to memories and hopes related to the deceased, until a final detachment enables the person's ego to become free and uninhibited again. According to Freud, a person's inability to disengage their psychic energy from a loved one and reinvest that energy elsewhere, such as in establishing new relationships, was a sign of illness.

Then, in 1920, Freud's youngest daughter, Sophie, died of Spanish flu, leaving behind two children and a husband. At that time, Freud seemingly applied a bit of his erroneous early theory about loss and mourning to himself. In a letter to a friend, Freud (2000b) wrote, "I work as much as I can, and am thankful for the diversion. The loss of a child seems to be a serious, narcissistic injury; what is known as mourning will probably follow only later" (p. 6).[2]

Freud's comments regarding his daughter's death seem intellectualized and far removed from what one would expect from a grief-stricken parent. In contrast, Freud clearly expressed grief when Sophie's son, Heinele, died from tuberculosis in June 1923. In a letter to Swiss psychiatrist Ludwig Binswanger in 1926, Freud revealed that since Heinele's death he "no longer [found] enjoyment in life" (Freud, 2003). Five years after his grandson's death, Freud professed in a letter to Ernest Jones that he "became tired of life permanently" when little Heinele died (Freud, 2000a). The loss of his close relationship with the child led him to consider the extreme painfulness of mourning and recognize the endlessness of normal grieving (Clewell, 2004).

Parents and grandparents who have experienced a child's death encounter profoundly sad reminders that the joy they once felt cannot be replicated. Episodic memories, which are designed to inform and prepare us for future events, instead activate sadness along with images of the child's lost opportunities. As an example, Janet assumed she had failed to grieve the loss of her son correctly because she experienced intense sadness every year on the anniversary of his death, on his birthday, and on all holidays. The Christmas ornaments he had made as a little boy had graced her tree every year, although the cutouts of Halloween pumpkins were now becoming a bit tattered, as was the pine cone paper-feathered turkey that served as a centerpiece for the Thanksgiving table. Now that 30 years had

---

[2]This highly influential framework became a template for how we mourn. Some psychoanalytic scholars (see Clewell, 2004) have suggested that Freud's true intention in that paper was to explore melancholia as a narcissistic disorder, because around that time he had introduced his theory of narcissism. Indeed, melancholia became accepted as a narcissistic identification with the hated aspects of an ambivalently loved person who has died.

passed since the loss, she wondered if it was possible to get over it and just let go. Unlike Freud, Janet found enjoyment in life, but, like him, she always carried the pain of her loss within her.

In an existential sense, some parents are able to access the child who still resides in memory and concurrently embrace what lives outside themselves. A couple who had lost their 10-year-old child to cancer took a trip 30 years later to Death Valley, California. Sitting on a rock and observing the vast desert, they watched the insects and the plants that grew opportunistically among the rocks. They relayed to me their conclusion that "there is so much life in Death Valley." One could assume that they have used autobiographical memories of loss to shape their perceptions in their present life.

MEMORY CONSOLIDATION

In an attempt to make sense of the day's experiences, the mind consolidates countless factual and autobiographical (explicit) recollections. These recollections are then combined with elements from the more distant past, including remembrances from past losses. In this process, generalities are extracted, multiple experiences are integrated, and memory traces over time are reorganized into a more permanent form for long-term storage (Wamsley & Stickgold, 2011). Some of this integration of memory and emotion occurs as we sleep and dream (Siegel, 2010; Zhao et al., 2018). It is not unusual to dream about someone who has died, or have a dream related to losing someone important to us, because their image may be activated by something that occurs in the present.

Remembering Through Dreams

Dreams are a combination of recent and past memories, leftover elements from the day's events, learning experiences, sensory input while we are asleep, and random images generated by the brain (Siegel, 2010; Wamsley & Stickgold, 2011; Zhao et al., 2018). The imagery of dreams is discussed in later chapters, so for now let's focus on what happens regarding our memories as we sleep and how this pertains to loss.

Rapid eye movement (also known as *REM*) sleep has been shown to play a role in emotional memory consolidation and the overall processing of emotional experiences in waking life (Scarpelli et al., 2019). A recent study of 216 individuals whose romantic partner or spouse had died found that grief dreams may be a way for people to regulate emotion, process trauma, and maintain a continuing bond with the deceased loved one (Black et al., 2021). Dreams of the deceased, according to the study authors, can help us adjust to bereavement.

In posttraumatic conditions, including those involving loss, memory processing during wakefulness or sleep may be impaired (Bower & Sivers, 1998; Siegel, 2001). When a blockage to consolidating memory occurs, the individual may experience intrusive images, flashbacks, and nightmares (Siegel, 2001). Because dreams that occur during rapid eye movement sleep play a role in processing emotional events and the consolidation of emotional memories, nightmares may represent a futile attempt of the brain to consolidate them (Scarpelli et al., 2019).

Dreaming and reporting dreams were significant in my relationship with my mother. The imagery in dreams fascinated her, and she often interpreted the dreams of our family members using a book her mother had brought with her when they had emigrated from Sicily. When we shared our dreams each morning, my mother would look up the symbolic meaning of the images and provide an Italian-to-English translation.

My mother's dream-divining skills were limited to the symbolic meanings offered by the author of the dream interpretation book, but symbols do have their place when it comes to understanding dreams. Many dream analysts are expansive in their use of symbolism. Jungian analysts, for example, consider an image of an elephant a clue that the dream has to do with one's mother. When I learned this symbolic translation much later in my life, I was intrigued because I had experienced a recurring "elephant dream" that persisted from early childhood until my preteen years:

I am awakened by the bellowing sound of an elephant. The elephant is charging down the hallway toward my bedroom at the end of the hall. A circus ringmaster is standing in the middle of the hallway between my parents' bedroom and the bathroom. He intercepts the elephant, swings it over his head by its trunk, and throws the elephant out of the bathroom window. I awaken frightened.

When I initially had the elephant dream, my mother wasn't home, so I told my father and brother, who then teased that I had dreamed about pink elephants. The elephant in my dream was solo, and it certainly wasn't pink, but their teasing provided a clue to the context of the dream. The night before we had seen the Disney movie *Dumbo*. In the film, crows tease a young elephant who thought he could fly. Later in the movie, the little elephant mistakenly drinks alcohol and, in his delirium, sees very scary pink elephants. I could understand why my brother and father associated my dream with the movie. Subsequently, though, when I would have the elephant dream my mother was home and would comfort me, much like Dumbo was comforted by his mother in the movie. This was the association that mattered.

In adulthood, my Freudian training analyst speculated that the recurring dream had to do with penis envy, or *primal scene* issues (see the "Useful Definitions" section at the end of this book), obviously having to do with the elephant's trunk and the fact that the scene took place in front of my parents' bedroom, respectively. However, the analyst had neglected essential elements of dream interpretation: She did not inquire about the circumstance under which my dream had initially occurred; neither had she considered the fact that I connected dreaming and the reporting of dreams with my mother. After becoming a mother myself, and while watching the movie *Dumbo* with my children, I realized that this dream had initially begun when my mother was hospitalized for cancer surgery. In an effort to distract my brother and me from her highly unusual absence, my father had taken us to see *Dumbo*, which is based on themes of separation and the terror of real or imagined loss.

Remembering Through Construction

As mentioned earlier in this chapter, although we believe what we remember is true to our experience, memory is not always accurate. I am not certain, for example, whether my elephant dream began during my mother's first hospitalization, when I was 4 years old, or during a second hospitalization, when I was 7. I assume the latter age is correct because children tend not to recall episodic memories before they are between 5 and 7 years old, although some early childhood memories with strong emotional content can be recalled (Richmond & Nelson, 2007).

In general, adults have trouble accessing early childhood episodic memories. Children lack a fully developed brain structure that enables long-term memory storage (McBride & Cutting, 2016). Adults who have lost a parent in their early childhood lament the absence of memories about their parent. This same type of deficit does not occur, though, with implicit memories and semantic memories (memories of basic facts, e.g., colors; McBride & Cutting, 2016). Therefore, aspects of relationships with parents remain stored in the child's implicit memory and inform their adulthood. So, although we may not consciously remember a loving parent, we are guided by our implicit memories of their nurturing.

Memory researchers regard *constructive memory* as a process that pieces together fragments of stored information that are influenced by current knowledge, attitudes, and beliefs (Schacter, 2012). Constructive memory uses the simulation of episodic memories to anticipate or predict the future. Thus, constructive memory represents an interaction between memory of past events and future predictions, including those of our future happiness (Schacter & Addis, 2007).

Forecasting the future is far more complex than predicting the weather, given that we have instruments that help us to foresee what the weather will be but none that let us look forward in time. The episodic memories that enable us to anticipate the future are not necessarily a reliable source. Past experiences may be highly memorable, but they may also be atypical or distorted (Loftus, 2003; Morewedge et al., 2007). Thus, to project ourselves into another time, place, or perspective involves not only remembering the past but also imagining the future.

Events reside in our memory as general-purpose knowledge, and when we are prompted to recall a specific situation we construct a transitory memory that changes slightly each time on the basis of situational demands (Bluck & Li, 2001). A few vivid details of an event may be recalled, but the accuracy of our recollection, as well as the significance of a memory, may diminish over time. Many events are initially recalled in a sensory form; thus, we may experience sensations associated with an event even though we may not be aware of the source of what we feel (Neisser & Harsch, 1992).

Humans are known to distort memories in ways that make the memory more consistent with their own biases, or they favor particular narratives that make sense to them (Gallo & Wheeler, 2013; H. M. Johnson & Seifert, 1994). When we have incorporated pieces of misinformation into our worldview or a larger narrative, we are likely to hold onto the misbeliefs more closely (H. M. Johnson & Seifert, 1994). Some aspects of loss and grief may lead us to favor what we most prominently want to recall, and in doing this we tend to overemphasize positive qualities of the deceased.

In some situations, we construct our memories around what fits for us or is comfortable at the time. When a loved one dies, our memories regarding their positive attributes may become amplified, muting memories of behaviors or personality traits we did not enjoy so much. We tend to idealize the departed. There are likely many elaborate psychological explanations for why we may be inclined to dismiss negative perceptions and amplify the positive. Because the future with someone who has died is nonexistent, memories about the less-than-positive traits of that person are not necessary to inform our future. Instead of focusing on negative qualities, which we may do when someone is alive, we can now attend only to positive qualities, such as those we remember from the distant past. We can thus let down our guard and love the lost person unconditionally.

On occasion, people put aside negative attitudes they have toward another person when they learn that their antagonist has become gravely ill or has died. As an example, upon hearing that her former husband was close to death, Noreen began to recall memories she had put behind her long ago. She became sad, remembering the love she had once felt for her ex-husband, despite the intense bitterness and animosity between them when their marriage had ended. She was hesitant to divulge her memories and conflicting feelings to close friends, especially given the 10 years they had supported her by alienating the husband who had left her. Now constructing her memories of the past around his good qualities, Noreen was tempted to call and thank her dying ex-spouse for the good times they had shared. Keeping her feelings to herself, she later attended his memorial service and said prayers for him.

The Trick of Constructive Memory

Constructive memory can "trick" us. Perhaps more accurately, I should say that my own constructive memory has tricked me. In the first chapter of this book, I described my occasional anticipatory anxiety that, like my mother, my life would be over at age 40-something. I had assumed that all of the knowledge I had gained from becoming a psychologist would prevent me from reacting when I eventually reached the age at which she died. Like my mother, though, I had also married at age 28, and my two children, like hers, were born 2.9 years apart. There was, however, an important difference: Whereas my mother had given birth to a boy and a girl, I had had two boys. I considered this difference as an omen that I could deceive fate.

More than a dozen years after my training and my work with the client who had experienced the significant anniversary reaction described in Chapter 1, I realized I was fast approaching my mother's age at death. Somewhat naïvely, I assumed I could prepare myself and avoid unpleasant surprises. At the time, I used similar logic when I anticipated encountering a mountain lion in predawn jogs on an isolated trail, protecting myself with hypervigilance and a body alarm.

Unlike the imagined mountain lion that might unexpectedly leap out from the bushes, however, the age-matching anniversary quietly prowled around my psyche and managed to distort my perceptions. Upon reaching my 42nd birthday, I knew I was getting close to my mother's age at her death. I looked through a box of documents saved in the back of a closet, which included her death certificate, photographs, prayer cards from her friends and relatives, and clippings about her death published in the small-town newspaper. Her birthday and mine are 3 days apart. Given that she died 2 weeks before her birthday, the calculations seemed easy. I concluded that if I made it to age 45, I should celebrate big time.

Thus, as my 45th birthday approached, I considered ritualizing the age-matching date. I mused about having a birthday party, because my later childhood birthdays had always seemed empty without my mother. Instead, I decided I would go to a church and light a candle for her.

Less than a month before the age-matching anniversary, I could not remember whether my mother had died on August 3rd or August 4th. Such obsessive thinking, I assumed, was my mind's way of diverting my distress away from the hope—and the guilt—that I would outlive her. Finally, I went into the closet, rummaged around, and pulled out the box of documents.

Upon opening the box, the first item I saw was her obituary, carefully cut from a newspaper. A surprising wave of unreality hit me. The bold heading noted her age at death as 43—she had actually died just before her 44th birthday. When I had read the clipping nearly 3 years earlier, I somehow perceived that she had died weeks before her 45th birthday. I frantically rifled through the other contents to validate my certainty of her age at death. Every record confirmed the newspaper article. The anniversary had passed nearly a year before.

I thought back to what had been happening around the time of the actual age-matching anniversary. The month before, I had started jogging and was surprised at how vibrant it made me feel. That same summer, I also decided to trade in my car, a station wagon befitting someone matronly, as I had always envisioned my mother, for a sports coupe with a sunroof. I had never felt so alive.

As I looked through several photos in the box, I realized that my mother was not always as matronly as my scattered childhood memories perceived her. I stared at a photograph of her standing on the steps of a church, wearing a silken black dress and stylish hat. In all likelihood, she was attending a funeral. In any case, my mom looked classy.

I turned toward my desk, opened the side drawer, and combed through paperwork to find a greeting card I had created the previous year without any intention of sending it to anyone. On the front of the card, in a soft and flowing font, I had written the first three lines of the poem "Holidays" by Henry Wadsworth Longfellow (1878):

> The holiest of all holidays are those
> Kept by ourselves in silence and apart;
> The secret anniversaries of the heart. (p. 96)

Laying the card on the old documents, I closed the top of the container and returned it to its place at the back of the closet.

TO SUMMARIZE

Memory is an adaptive process that enables us to use past experiences and information to imagine present and future possibilities. The experience of grief involves a comparison of the present with the contents of our memories. Many different kinds of memories interface with experiences of loss, including implicit, explicit, episodic, emotional, and autobiographical memories. A narrative self-definition is created by our accumulated autobiographical memories, along with our future intentions. A significant loss alters both the narrative of our lives and the sense of continuity within our autobiographical memories. Although autobiographical memories can help prepare us for what is to come, the sense of discontinuity resulting from the loss of a loved one means we have to learn how to revise the future we have planned. Dreams are a combination of recent and past memories, leftover elements from the day's events, learning experiences, sensory input while we sleep, and random images generated by our brain. They help us adjust to loss. Finally, part of being human is that our memories may sometimes be flawed, distorted, or inaccurate.

Our sense of self and our identity are created through the synthesis of a lifetime of memories. If who we are is intertwined with someone who dies, our sense of self may be rocked. Chapter 3 explores the concepts of self and identity in self-defining memories, attachment, and prolonged grief.

Reflections

- When a pleasant memory evokes the sadness of loss, try to stay with the enjoyment you felt with that person at the time while not dismissing your sadness.
- How do you cope with triggering events related to loss? What strategies do you use to take care of your emotional well-being?

CHAPTER 3

LOSS, IDENTITY, AND
OUR SENSE OF SELF

*Divorce was a rare and forbidden deed in my young life and Catholic
upbringing. Nonetheless, as my mother explained, my beloved Uncle
Orazio and his wife had divorced "because she fed him out of cans."
I wondered how canned food was a greater sin than divorce. Uncle
Orazio preferred to eat vegetables and fruit he had grown in his
large garden, a plot surrounded by stacks of pancaked vehicles in the
middle of his auto wrecking yard, so her justification seemed plausible. Uncle Orazio remarried the year before my mother's death. My
new aunt, Hope, who was sensual, smart, and opinionated, worked
as a butcher—an unusual occupation for a woman at the time. Her
skills likely were handy whenever Uncle Orazio slaughtered one of
the chickens that pecked around the wrecking yard garden.*

*After my mother died, one of my aunts proposed altering some of
my mother's dresses for me to wear, given my family's modest income.
Aunt Hope insisted that the clothes were not right for a young girl
and later took me shopping for new school clothes. Her taste differed
considerably from my mother's, and wearing the clothes seemed to
alter how I perceived myself. The year after my mother's death, Aunt
Hope died tragically in a fiery automobile accident on her way to work.
In a nearly unimaginable irony, Uncle Orazio, who volunteered as a
fireman, had been called to the horrible scene. I always worried about*

the pain that must have lived within his heart. I wish I could have told him that I wanted to be someone like Aunt Hope.

Our identity and sense of self are shaped by the synthesis of memories accumulated during a lifetime. Within our recollections are images of people we have known and lost, along with the emotions we felt during our shared experiences with them. Through remembering, we enfold the people we have loved, and who have loved us, into who we become. Memories link our past relationships to our present identity, and we take them with us as we craft the future we imagine for ourselves. They are a framework for the abbreviated and extended narratives of our life story.

You may recall from the previous chapter that Endel Tulving (2007) noted that 256 different kinds of memory had been described by researchers, so you probably won't be surprised if I introduce another form of memory to you: Meet *self-defining memory*, a subset of autobiographical memory. Self-defining memory involves life-story reference points. This interesting form of memory also encompasses scenes of a remembered self in relation to someone who has passed, as well as to the significance of their passing.

This chapter focuses on how loss affects our self-definition and identity. First, though, it is important to figure out what is meant by the "self" in reference to concepts like a sense of self, self-esteem, self-consciousness, self-image, self-respect, self-disgust, or self-defining memories. Furthermore, what is the role of autobiographical memory in determining our sense of self and how we construct a personal identity?

THE SELF, SELF-DEFINING MEMORIES, AND IDENTITY

Intrinsic to the concept of a self is *consistency*—a sense of sameness and continuity—despite change or growth (James, 1890/1950; Nathanson, 1992). From infancy onward, our sense of self forms in interpersonal contexts that create our personal attributes and becomes a personal, subjective awareness. This awareness includes a sense of agency, continuity, and emotional vitality (Basten & Touyz, 2020). Much of how we experience ourselves in the world involves the continuous autobiographical memories that make up our *narrative self* (Gallagher, 2000).

Like "sense of self," the word "identity" conveys a sameness or oneness; however, "identity" refers to the absolute or essential sameness in the substance, nature, composition, or properties that are attached to a person or thing (Nathanson, 1992). It describes a person's self-perception through cognitive self-awareness and their commitments to beliefs and values (Basten & Touyz, 2020).

Recollections affect how we view our self, just as much as our sense of self influences how we recall the past (Wilson & Ross, 2003). Significant losses can contribute to—or even alter—how we experience ourselves. For example, numerous episodic memories of loss scripted the narrative of my own life story. Being a motherless daughter and, later, a fatherless daughter, played a role in my sense of self and identity in early adulthood. When I looked at the past, memories of my parents became reminders of loss, and they helped me understand how I became my self. As an adult, losing a spouse temporarily altered my sense of identity and personal consistency, even though, in many other ways, I view myself as the same person I was before his death. An altered self-perception is apparent in relationships to coupled friends I had shared with my husband, but not in my relationships with individuals. In any case, my loss has become a *self-defining memory*.

Throughout our lives, some memories carry more emotional intensity and vividness than others. They play like movie scenes in our heads, and we tend to recall them repetitively as touchstones or reference points in our lives (Singer & Blagov, 2004). These self-defining memories become linked to other similar memories; together, they tend to be focused on an enduring concern, or they relate to an unresolved conflict, or they give us insights into the kaleidoscopic picture of ourselves (Singer & Blagov, 2004). These key episodes from childhood to late adulthood create the chapters of our story and illuminate the major themes in our lives (Singer, 2019; Singer & Blagov, 2004). They may involve our connection with others, times when we overcame adverse circumstances, and times when life events gave us insight or allowed us to make meaning of something. Self-defining memories carry an emotional charge, adding an intense positive or negative value to our reconstruction of past events (Singer & Blagov, 2004). They can also unsettle our rational understanding of past experiences, and they can intensify the importance of similar current events (Singer & Blagov, 2004).

Autobiographical memories enhance our feelings of personal consistency through time and play a role in constructing a personal identity (Wilson & Ross, 2003). We become the author of our identity as we create a life story; link together present, past, and future aspects of the self; and attach a sense of purpose to how we behave and think (McAdams, 1987). Thus, the characteristics that define us, that set our identity, are imbued with a quality of sameness through time.

The concept of identity and the theory of identity formation that became a mainstay in psychology is primarily attributed to the work of Erik H. Erikson. As it is with many human development theories, the concept of identity was personal to Erikson and based on his own disenfranchised loss (a loss that may not appear worthy of grief; Doka, 1989). In essence, Erikson's exploration of identity was motivated by his longing to know his biological father. He was born as the result of an extramarital liaison between his mother and a man whose name his mother refused to reveal throughout Erikson's life. She gave young Erik the surname of her second husband, and throughout Erik's early life he believed that his stepfather was his biological father (Friedman, 1999). As an adult, searching for his own identity, he changed his name from Erik Homburger to Erik Homburger Erikson. The mystery of his biological father's identity resulted in Erikson's confusion about his own and led him to pursue a scholarly inquiry that helped us all understand identity.

> **Loss may lead us to question the ways in which we belong and whether or not others will accept us.**

Along with answering the basic question of who we are, identity also involves a sense of belonging and acceptance, in contrast to feelings of rejection or self-disgust (Plutchik, 2013). Loss may lead us to question the ways in which we belong and whether or not others will accept us given the changes that have taken place in us and in our lives. An important part of Sarah's adult life, for example, involved activities with her husband. Their shared knowledge of botany and their outings to unusual places were an essential part of her story about herself. When her husband suddenly died, for many months Sarah felt as though part of her identity, connected to the future she anticipated she would share with her husband, also disappeared. The thought of socializing as a threesome with friends and their partners felt awkward and uncomfortable to Sarah, as though part of herself would be missing in their interactions. At times, an intense sense of loneliness enveloped her. She questioned who she was without her partner.

In a different way, the continuity of Emily's sense of identity was temporarily disrupted by her husband's death. Emily's husband had sometimes teased that their mutual friends had all come from his social circle before their marriage. As a high-achieving, confident professional, Emily claimed that she never took him seriously, but after he died she questioned who she was without him, wondering if these long-term friends would stay in her life without her husband's presence. When we grieve, it is often difficult to tell whether we are bereft over the loss of another person or over the loss of a part of our sense of self or identity in relation to them.

ATTACHMENT, IDENTITY, AND SELF-DEFINITION

Psychologist John Archer (1999) proposed that grief is a by-product of human attachment, a price we pay "for being able to love in the way we do" (p. 5). However, Archer maintained that because grief compels us to search for the person who was lost, it is a maladaptive pattern of commitment. In other words, our attachment to the deceased may lead us to refuse commitment to other people worthy of it, or to seek commitment from those unable to reciprocate. Both situations add pain to what we have lost and hope to recover again. Perhaps our searching and longing to restore our connection with a deceased loved one are not maladaptive, yet they can still be painful. In Chapter 4, we explore how such searching makes sense in terms of memory processes.

> **The experience of grief may vary according to the emotional strength of the lost relationship.**

For now, let's consider the question of whether our experience of grief varies according to the emotional strength of the lost relationship. Unfortunately, some points of view tend to emphasize that dependency on love and validation through a partner are unhealthy and result in prolonged grief symptoms that include longing, preoccupation with the deceased, significant functional impairment, and emotional distress that persist beyond 6 months (World Health Organization, 2022). In some cases, that may be true; however, issues of attachment and loss are very complex. Nevertheless, some theorists have proposed that the security of a relationship serves to help people avoid shame and attachment fear and thus that a prolonged grieving period may signify the failure of an individual's avoidance strategy (Dellmann, 2018; Shear et al., 2007). In such situations, the loss of the emotional connection with the deceased loved one requires cognitive reorganization that will help the person find ways to connect with others. However, it's not easy to replace someone to whom we have been deeply attached. Many studies based on attachment theories indicate that people for whom deep attachment and dependency fostered a sense of emotional security are most vulnerable to grief problems when the person with whom they were entwined dies or disappears (Fraley & Bonanno, 2004; Maccallum & Bryant, 2008). Individuals who developed a dependent attachment style early in life tend to form later relationships that are concentrated on one person, and that person satisfies their need for human bonding (Archer, 1999; Parkes & Weiss, 1983; Prigerson et al., 1997). As a result, the attached person experiences profound and prolonged grief when that person dies.

Emotional attachment is a complex process. A strong connection flows from an emotional resonance between two individuals. We often hear people with a strong emotional bond claiming they and their beloved finish each other's sentences or know what the other is thinking. This process, often referred to by psychologists as *interaffectivity*, involves unconscious communication between two people whereby their brains rapidly appraise and perceptually process emotional cues. Nonverbal communication involves even the unconscious perception of movements in the regions around the eyes (Schore, 2012). Prosodic elements of communication, such as vocal tones and rhythms, also make voices into instruments of emotional expression; they allow us to convey emotional messages to others (Schore, 2012).

A close bond creates both lingering grief and a reminder of the power of love.

EVOLVING THEORIES

Close friendships, marriages, partnerships, and various romantic entanglements involve strong bonds of attachment, yet the bonds we once experienced with someone can form a ghost that haunts us after they die. Shakespeare's 30th Sonnet, written more than 400 years ago, reveals his sadness about losing a dear friend, a sadness that always returned as he remembered the past (Shakespeare, 1609/2008). He noted that his sorrow had dulled over the years and expressed regret about wasting precious time replaying old woes in his mind instead of indulging in positive thoughts. Yet he concluded that sweet recollections of his dear friend always compensated for the pain of his sorrow.

Centuries after Shakespeare illustrated how a close bond creates both lingering grief and a reminder of the power of love, our efforts to understand how people become attached to others and later respond to loss led to the notion that we simply work through grief and get over it. This notion is confusing and lacks Shakespeare's nuance and ambiguity, which come closer to human experience. In 1952, attachment theorists John Bowlby and James Robertson conceptualized mourning phases on the basis of children's reaction to separation and loss (Bowlby et al., 1952). Later, Bowlby and his colleague Colin Murray Parkes (1970) applied these phases to the study of bereavement in adults. The attachment perspective they offered viewed continued bonds as serving essential functions: An ongoing internal relationship to the image of the deceased, this view holds, is an important aspect of mourning and a normal part of healthy adaptation. This understanding that grief stays with us and is valuable transforms our view of it.

> **Grief does not have defined stages, and relinquishing our attachment to a loved one is not central to the task of mourning.**

Early in her career, Elisabeth Kübler-Ross was interested in attachment theory in her attempts to further an understanding of death and dying. At first, she created a *stage theory model* that she applied to death and dying that was similar to Bowlby's conceptualization (Kübler-Ross, 1969). In 1969, Kübler-Ross published her stage theory model, which viewed grief as a process whereby closure is achieved by traversing five prescribed stages: (a) denial, (b) anger, (c) bargaining, (d) depression, and (e) acceptance (Kübler-Ross & Kessler, 2014). This conceptualization was later widely refuted; nonetheless, it became a dominant model for the pattern of adjustment in how we grieve. Although many people may identify with the behaviors and stages Kübler-Ross proposed, the theory has little to do with how people respond to loss and cope with it. However, the sequence of stages she described remains in many people's minds because it offers a sense of predictability over the unpredictable (Lilienfeld et al., 2010).

We now understand that grief does not have defined stages, and relinquishing attachments to the departed is not central to the task of mourning. There are many ways to navigate loss. The many different ways we traverse loss are influenced by our past and present circumstances; the nature of our emotional intimacy with the departed;

and our culture, beliefs, resilience, and available support systems. We each have a unique response.

People cope with loss differently, and for many this involves a very silent remembering.

Although some people move through their grief rather quickly, others' journey is much longer. Couples who experience a common loss in their lives seem to demonstrate these differences. Whereas one partner may want to isolate, the other may want to be around many people. Someone who values the expression of feelings may believe a partner does not feel similarly if the partner does not talk about the loss or recount memories of the person who has died. As individuals, we cope in different ways. For many people, this involves a very silent remembering.

Some researchers have speculated that the griever's ambivalent relationship to the lost loved one affects their self-appraisal and ability to cope without the beloved (N. P. Field & Sundin, 2001). But is ambivalence what accounts for this effect on the griever? More recent research has emphasized the concept of *merged identity*, namely, that people with an identity constructed around the deceased loved one have a more disrupted identity after loss and more difficulty integrating the loss into their lives than those with an independent identity (Badia, 2019; Maccallum & Bryant, 2013). However, the notion that grief is linked to a merged identity disregards that a loving connection with someone is complex and difficult to relinquish. For example, Julia stated,

> I lost my husband to lung cancer 4 months ago. He was 49 years old. I grieve him every single day, almost all the time. The pain

and the feeling of loss and being cheated [are] always there. I feel cheated that he didn't get to live a longer life and that I am left all alone, desperately missing him with all my being. I hope and pray that over time my pain will lessen and I will learn to adapt to this new life without the love of my life.

An independent identity is thought to involve an individual's self-perceptions, goals, and motivations that are not entirely based on the deceased. Grief, however, is considered to be an experience of identity disruption regardless of whether a person has an independent identity. A grieving person's attempts to maintain a connection with the deceased may elicit anxiety and subsequent maladaptive behaviors, such as excessive alcohol consumption, in response to loss (Bonanno et al., 2001; Bowlby, 1980). Paradoxically, some research has indicated that merged identity, such as that which happens in a long and interdependent marriage, can lead to identity continuity and less severe grief. In other words, maintaining a continuing bond through recollection and ritual might be beneficial for individuals with a merged identity, compared with those who have a merged identity and thus cannot maintain a connection (Badia, 2019).

Maintaining a continuing bond through recollection and ritual might be beneficial for some people.

IDENTITY AND PROLONGED GRIEF

A study of bereaved adults who had lost a spouse found that people who suffered complex grief had difficulty recalling specific events from the past as well as imagining particular events in the future that would not include their deceased partner (Robinaugh & McNally,

49

2013). The researchers speculated that these difficulties might be explained by a sense of lost identity and hopelessness. Moreover, difficulty envisioning the future without the deceased may provide the basis for symptoms of yearning. People who experience *complicated grief*, an alternative term for prolonged grief, tend to have more self-defining memories and intense feelings of yearning because their self-identity is so strongly related to the deceased (Conway & Pleydell-Pearce, 2000; Maccallum & Bryant, 2008). It is possible they yearn for the self that found expression in their relationship.

Part of my father's sense of self and identity seemed lost after my mother's death. He seemed to lack enjoyment, and he neglected activities that had brought him pleasure in the past, such as his woodworking projects. When death ruptures the interpersonal bond between individuals, building a bond with someone new can transcend the emotion of shame that is activated by disconnection (Kaufman, 1974). Ideally, a bridge is restored and a new bond provides an opportunity for the bereaved person to restore a sense of self and continuity in life. In his heart, though, my father had no motivation to replace my mother.

Urging my father to "move on" from his grief, perhaps for the sake of finding someone who would take care of his children, my mother's brother, Uncle Orazio, encouraged my father to date. Given that my uncle had found the love of his life, Aunt Hope, after a divorce from his first wife, he sought someone appropriate for my father. In fact, he introduced my 44-year-old father to a woman of a similar age who had never dated. Within the year, my father announced to my brother and me that he would marry this woman, adding that it was because he felt sorry for her and could not abandon her. Soon after their marriage, my new stepmother, perhaps enraged by my father's unspoken and continued attachment to his dead wife, became physically and emotionally abusive to us. Although the abuse was unknown to Uncle Orazio, he was aware of my stepmother's erratic personality and my father's unhappiness, and he urged my father to divorce her. For my father, though, divorce was out of the question.

Holding my mother close to my heart, I managed to maintain my self-definition despite constant hostility from my stepmother. Memories of my mother and others who had loved me helped me focus my attention on a more desirable future and, like my father, I tried to empathize with this psychologically disturbed woman. In the face of adversity, memories can protect us, enhancing our feelings of personal consistency through time (Wilson & Ross, 2003).

Perhaps looking toward the future was also a way out for my father, although that imagined next step did not include my stepmother. I suspect he was resolute that leaving his rheumatic heart disease untreated would enable him to die and to join my mother in heaven. Culture defines the significance of certain events, the shape of a life, and the framework for understanding those experiences (Fivush, 2018; McLean & Syed, 2015). Nevertheless, by today's standards my father would likely be diagnosed as having a persistent and pervasive grief response, now commonly referred to as "prolonged grief disorder," "complicated grief," or "persistent complex bereavement disorder."

The World Health Organization (2022) defined prolonged grief disorder thus:

> [a disturbance] characterized by longing for the deceased or persistent preoccupation with the deceased accompanied by intense emotional pain (e.g.[,] sadness, guilt, anger, denial, blame, difficulty accepting the death, feeling one has lost a part of one's self, an inability to experience positive mood, emotional numbness, difficulty in engaging with social or other activities).[1]

---

[1]Diagnostic guidelines provided in the World Health Organization's *International Statistical Classification of Diseases and Related Health Problems* include prolonged grief disorder as a diagnosis in the forthcoming 11th edition, to be published in January 2022.

The criteria for the disorder also specify that the grief response has persisted for more than 6 months; exceeds the norms for the individual's culture and context; and that the disturbance causes significant impairment in personal, family, social, educational, and occupational functioning.

Prolonged grief disorder is thought to involve distinctive autobiographical memory patterns related to the individual's self-definition (Maccallum & Bryant, 2008). For example, Catherine, 52, had called her mother every day of her life, and those conversations shaped her understanding of daily experiences: of her daughter's process of maturing, of successes at work, or her friendships. The conversations shaped her ideas about who she was in the world. When her mother died, she couldn't "get [her] groove back."

People whose stories are heavily intertwined with the deceased, as Catherine's was, are more likely to view their self-identity as closely linked with the deceased than bereaved people who do not meet the criteria for prolonged grief disorder (Bellet, LeBlanc, et al., 2020; J. G. Johnson et al., 2006; Maccallum & Bryant, 2008). Focusing attention on the absence of their loved one activates feelings of yearning and distress, because these people are more likely than other bereaved individuals to recall memories that involve the "lost self" (Maccallum & Bryant, 2008).

A parent's identity is so intertwined with that of their child or children that losing a child can be a devastating experience. Consider Olivia, who responded to a blog post I wrote about grief being something we do not get over:

> When a so-called "friend" told me the loss of my 17-year-old son would make me stronger over time, I turned and walked away. After 25 years, I can testify that doesn't happen, and I can't believe anyone who has experienced the death of a child would say anything good came of it. Yes, I lead an active life, laugh frequently, and love more, but any little thing can take me back to that horrible

moment. Grief isn't something you get over. It's something you learn to live with. Articles that tell you that you will "grow" after loss or that list three dozen ways to "overcome" your grief are actually insulting and hurtful. I don't want to grow, become stronger, or move on. I'd rather be weak and have my child back.

Ten percent to 15% of people suffer from prolonged grief and complicated grief (Boyraz et al., 2015; Neimeyer & Thompson, 2014). Among my clients, grief is certainly more intense and complicated when they lost a loved one to whom they were deeply connected. Granted, recognizing very extreme grief as a disorder has an upside, such as making insurance coverage possible for those who seek psychotherapy or medical assistance. In some cases, recognizing that one has an identifiable diagnosis can lead them to feel their distress and suffering are finally understood and can be treated. However, the existence of these diagnoses may encourage the misunderstanding that grief is something we need to get over. It is not. Grief is something we need to live with creatively.

In an attempt to make sense of the differences between recovery from grief and long-term bereavement, researchers have primarily focused on dependency, attachment styles, and the capacity for resilience (Carr et al., 2000; Denckla et al., 2011; Fraley & Bonanno, 2004). Factors such as interpersonal dependency, an avoidant or anxious attachment style, and limited resilience certainly may contribute to later complex grief symptoms. One often-overlooked dimension of long-term bereavement involves relationships between "soul mates."

LOSS OF A SOUL MATE

Samantha, who lost her soul mate after 36 years, explained that she and her partner, Carlton, had lived for each moment together. Nobody in her life seemed to understand her sense of losing herself upon losing her partner. Rituals between Samantha and Carlton were embedded in her memories. *She recalled how every day, upon her return home from work, Carlton embraced her and inquired about her day. Now that he was gone, she imagined conversations with him, although these episodes often ended with a sad recognition of his absence. Samantha's sister told her it was time to move on, yet Samantha had no intention of letting go of her soul mate.*

The term "soul mate" implies a special affinity for, understanding of, or powerful bond between one person and another. In many ways, a soul mate relationship contributes to our self-definition, both in reality and in memory after a partner's death. The experience of being known by and knowing another lends itself to the mythical image of two wandering souls finally reuniting. Outside of myth, however, the soul mate experience involves the sharing of emotional and subjective experiences. This is also called "interaffectivity" or "intersubjectivity" (Schore, 2012).

Researchers have found that romantic love can and does persevere in long-term relationships, and it is associated with well-being, satisfaction, and high self-esteem (Acevedo & Aron, 2009). The echoing of intellectual and personal interests can bind two people together as soul mates. The resonance that takes place between two minds who experience mutual interests allows the self to grow (Bromberg, 2009). Mutual excitement and enjoyment of sexual intimacy promote interest and novelty—emotions that would promote long-term satisfaction in a relationship—yet interest and novelty may also be the result of shared excitement and joy.

> **Navigating grief may be far more complicated if we are involved in a soul mate relationship that shapes our self-concept.**

The old saying that pets resemble the people who own them may apply to people in soul mate relationships in terms of incorporating features of a loved one into the self (Aron et al., 1995). We resemble the people we love and who love us. Theorists refer to the idea that people in a close relationship may experience a cognitive overlapping of their self-concepts, whereby features of the other are subsumed into one's own self-knowledge, and they may even confuse the self with the close other (Mashek et al., 2003; Swann & Bosson, 2010). Thus, navigating grief may be far more complicated if we are involved in a soul mate relationship that shapes our self-concept. Psychiatrist Colin Murray Parkes (2015) described the pain of grief as "just as much a part of life as the joy of love; it is, perhaps, the price we pay for love, the cost of commitment" (p. 1).

So, how do people unravel their sense of self and identity from a soul mate who dies? A reader of a blog post I wrote about grief wondered if she had done something wrong in immersing herself in work and furthering her education:

> When my soul mate and husband of 32 years died 17 years ago, I coped by working long hours . . . and worked on a degree at nights. I still feel overwhelming waves of grief at unexpected moments and have often wondered whether by coping in that way and not letting myself stay home and mourn I did the wrong thing. Emotional loss is indeed something for which there is no closure. Just learning to acknowledge the triggers and let[ting] the wave of emotion pass through is enough.

Discovering and maintaining a new consistency in one's sense of self helps us continue to live fully, and we should trust that waves of emotion will pass.

Whether this reader had let herself stay home and grieve or returned to work would not have erased the emotional triggers reminding her of her loss. Her advice is sound: We should trust that a wave of emotion will pass. A new challenge, such as work, further education, or volunteering becomes uniquely one's own experience, separate from a partner. Overlapping experience incorporates a loved one into one's sense of self and identity, whereas novel solo experiences (regardless of whether they also involve other people) helps one reestablish a separate sense of self. Without judging how people cope with loss, we can say that discovering and maintaining a new consistency in one's sense of self when a loved one dies helps us continue to live fully.

TO SUMMARIZE

The synthesis of our lifetime of memories is instrumental in creating our sense of self and our identity. In this chapter, we have explored the concept of self-defining memory, a subset of autobiographical memory. We took a look at the concepts of self and identity concerning self-defining memories, attachment, and prolonged grief. We considered how the progressive decline of a loved one may affect one's sense of self, physical health, relationships, and behavior.

Emotions and emotional memories are key elements of grief. In the next chapter, we look at the complex and sometimes confusing ways that these play out when we experience loss.

Reflections

- How did your sense of identity interface with a loved one, and how has it been altered in response to their loss? What steps can you take (or what steps have you taken) to re-create your self-definition?
- Because grief does not have defined stages, how would you describe your own unique experience of grief, the ways in which it has changed, and what you expect as time passes?

CHAPTER 4

FEELING OUR MEMORIES

As a motherless preadolescent, I dreaded expressions of sympathy or pity from well-intentioned people. Solicitudes produced toxic ripples of shame within me. Keeping my loss hidden was challenging. When door-to-door salesmen asked for my mother, I took cover behind a simple truth, claiming, "She isn't home." Strangely, while she was living, my mother occasionally instructed me to tell the frequent peddlers those same words.

Outside my front door, the awkward embarrassment about being motherless affected me most. On the first day of middle school, a friend introduced me as, "This-is-Mary-her-mother-just-died." Another friend nervously explained that she could not visit me any-more because I didn't have a mother. Unable to find words for what I felt, I assured the school counselor, who had asked to meet with me, that everything was fine. Such situations unveiled an elusive inner sense of lacking something critically important and an ineffable longing for what was missing.

The process of adapting to loss is a subjective emotional experience.

The process of adapting to loss is a subjective emotional experience. Grieving involves our memories of an attachment to someone and our responses to physical detachment from them. When positive emotional memories commingle with the reality of loss, we experience the bittersweetness of longing or the emptiness of depression. Reminders of enjoyable events, exciting interactions, or comical situations we have shared with someone who has died may result in sadness rather than the pleasant nostalgia we felt when reminiscing with them about the past.

As mentioned in Chapter 3, emotions felt by grieving individuals are often silently held. Many adults (as well as children) who have experienced loss hide what they remember and feel for many different reasons; among those reasons is to avoid judgment or being perceived as burdensome. As a result, we often convey facts rather than emotions about our loss. For example, my teenage autobiographical narrative that opens this chapter involved being a motherless daughter. I could have chosen instead to report the factual information of when and how my mother died while scarcely feeling the lived experience of losing her. This would have been a safer option, emotionally.

> **The emotional states of grief are often shadowed by impossible motives, such as restoring a connection with the person who is gone, or tempering our regrets.**

Emotions alert us to opportunities, problems, and what's going on around us as we traverse the present and prepare for the future. They draw our attention to something in positive, negative, or neutral ways and motivate a response. However, the emotional states of grief are often shadowed by impossible goals, such as restoring a connection with the person who is gone, or tempering our regrets. During the weeks that follow a significant loss, even the smallest joys that we cannot share with the lost loved one convert to sadness. As an example, I became tearful upon seeing the ripened loquats on the tree my husband and I had planted from a seed—a reminder that he is not here to taste them with me. Grief is always deeply personal and particular. Making sense of what we feel and deriving meaning from what has happened may seem more than we can manage emotionally, and yet there are ways to emotionally reinvest in the various meanings life offers us.

EMOTIONAL MEMORIES AND THE EXPERIENCE OF GRIEF

As Kevin and his wife settled into their theater seats, Kevin began feeling anxious and found himself focused on an elderly couple seated in the row in front of them. Suddenly, he desperately needed air. Excusing himself and rushing along the aisle, Kevin fled toward the nearest exit and, once outside, took some deep breaths. Unable to tamp down his panic, he headed for the parking garage. Disoriented and overwhelmed, he locked himself inside the car and began weeping. As Kevin regained his composure, he tried to make sense of what had happened. He remembered that nearly a year ago he had purchased tickets for his elderly parents to attend an event at this same theater. Kevin's mother had attended the event with a friend because his father had insisted on staying home. At home alone that evening, Kevin's father had died by suicide. Kevin's emotional memories, triggered by sitting in the theater and seeing the older couple, were reminders of the overwhelming helplessness he had experienced when his father had died.

As mentioned in Chapter 2, the term *emotional memory* describes the effects of emotion on episodic memory and refers to a consciously remembered experience that activates an emotional reaction. Thus, emotional memories are those that are related to emotional events or to stimuli that occurred in an emotional context (Buchanan & Adolphs, 2004). Any situation or circumstance in the present that matches a past memory, or even a gist of a memory, can reactivate emotions that were felt at the time. When these emotions surface, however, we may not make this connection and thus struggle to understand why we feel as we do.

> **Memories involving emotional events have a distinct persistence and vividness.**

Memories involving emotional events have distinct persistence and vividness (Phelps, 2004). For instance, we may emotionally reexperience some of the selective details of high-arousal information, such as a particular moment during a loved one's suffering (Buchanan & Adolphs, 2004; Kensinger & Schacter, 2016).[1] The vividness of details is influenced by the emotions we felt at the time as well as by the personal meaning the experience held for us. An example from my own life involves the memory of finding my husband partially conscious after his stroke. Some of the details of that event, such as the wincing of his mouth, empty gaze, and labored breathing, are attached to the shock of witnessing him in that state. The memory persisted in the early weeks after his loss, and each time I reminded

---

[1]During emotional arousal, the amygdala (a region of the brain's medial temporal lobe) is engaged and influences other areas in the brain involved with the processing and retention of nonarousing stimuli and regions that modulate memory, including the hypothalamus; hippocampus; and the cingulate, insular, and orbitofrontal cortices.

myself that it was just one horrible, yet significant, moment among all my memories of him.

Many of us have encountered situations when our memory of an event does not quite match another person's memory of what occurred. The emotions experienced by each individual at the time, as well as the thoughts associated with what is felt, may account for this discrepancy. As previously described, our recollections may or may not be accurate. Emotions can bias our attention, leading to *preferential perceptions*—predispositions to attend to certain things over others (Todd et al., 2012). In this sense, we seem to have a built-in emotional filtering process that adjusts our responses to situations and events and how we remember them.

As a result, the fact that controversy exists about the accuracy of memory should come as little surprise. Past studies have found that the accuracy of memories can be distorted (when we have confidence in a memory that proves to be inaccurate) and that memory can be manipulated (e.g., whether or not false memories of childhood events can be implanted; Buchanan & Adolphs, 2004). More recently, though, researchers have found that memory is malleable but essentially reliable; that false memories cannot be easily implanted; and that the accuracy of remembered details remains high with age, even though some details will fade along with recall of the actual sequence of past events (Brewin et al., 2020; Diamond et al., 2020; Diamond & Levine, 2020). In any case, when we lose someone we love, our relationship with that person continues through our memories of them, distorted or not. As a therapist, would I care whether or not your memories of a loved one are reliable? Actually, no. We grieve on the basis of what we have personally experienced and have come to believe; that is, the relationship we had with someone is an image that lives within us that is based on our remembered experiences. So, the way someone lives within us is subject to our biases and perceptions from the beginning of our relationship with them.

EMOTIONS

Because my goal in this book is to provide you with psychological insight into grief, I first have to provide a bit of information about emotions and how they work. What emotions lie at the core of what we feel, and how do they transform us on the basis of the experiences, culture, and the environment in which we live? Which of our primary emotions create grief and other grief-related experiences, such as a sense of longing?

All of us share a similar biological basis for our emotions, but we differ in the psychology of our emotions. Theorists use various words to refer to the unconscious biological source of emotions, including "affect," "primary emotion," "basic emotion," and "core emotion." When an emotion is activated at a biological level, our nervous system creates physiological and sensory responses in our body. Our cognitive system instantaneously scans our memories of past experiences to form thoughts and images that accompany an emotion and provide it with meaning. So, whereas one person may respond to shame by withdrawing, another person may attack others. Along with cognition and memory, the subsystems of perception, motor control, and language make more specific what the emotion conveys. Although there is a commonality to what we feel, our individual psychology influences how we respond to certain feelings. Emotional responses are influenced by personal history, the culture in which we were raised, the place we live, the way we have learned to express emotion, and how others have responded to our emotional expressions. As a result, the experience of grief differs among people according to the ways their past histories have scripted their emotional responses.

Primary and Core Emotions and Emotional States

Grief is an emotional state based on a combination of *primary* (basic or core) *emotions* (affects). Classification systems of emotions vary among emotion theorists. I will cite just a few of these to provide you with some idea of the differences, which are not vast. Perhaps you can guess where the emotions involved in your own experience of grief would derive from each of them.

One example is the taxonomy developed by Silvan Tomkins (2008), a psychologist and personality theorist. Tomkins considers the range of emotional expression, from mild to intense, and thus ascribes two-word names to identify most emotions (affects) within his classification system. These nine biologically based primary affects are (a) interest–excitement, (b) enjoyment–joy, (c) surprise–startle, (d) fear–terror, (e) distress–anguish, (f) anger–rage, (g) shame–humiliation, (h) disgust, and (i) dissmell (a unique name for toxic or bad smells). Another major classification system of emotions is based on the work of psychologist Paul Ekman (2003). Using distinctive universal facial expressions to form his classification system, Ekman focuses on the behavioral basis of emotions. He considers the seven core emotions to include (a) anger, (b) disgust, (c) fear, (d) happiness, (e) surprise, (f) contempt, and (g) sadness. Shame is not included as a core emotion because Ekman could not test shame as having a universal facial expression; instead, it is subsumed within the emotion of sadness. We know today, however, that shame is expressed bodily through a loss of muscle tone in the neck and shoulders, a downcast face, an averted gaze, and an initial sense of confusion known as *cognitive shock*. Yet another well-known theorist, Antonio Damasio, regards fear, happiness, anger, disgust, surprise, and sadness as core emotions (Damasio, 2000).

Aside from these biologically based emotions, there is an expansive array of other emotions we may feel at a given time, and this is especially the case when we are grieving. We may experience two or more primary emotions, whereby one activates in close proximity to another or whereby one emotion is triggered in response to another. In such cases, we experience the effects of an *emotional state*, such as anxiety, longing, depression, love, or grief.

> **A fundamental principle about how we function emotionally is that we are motivated to do something on the basis of our desire to turn on positive emotions or turn off negative ones.**

People in the throes of grieving understandably want to restore the positive emotions that feel rewarding, that bring interest and enjoyment into their lives. Although we value positive emotions, classifying primary emotions as positive or negative has little to do with their importance to us; instead, it involves how they *motivate* us through the ways they make us feel. A fundamental principle about how we function emotionally is that we are motivated to do something on the basis of our desire to turn on positive emotions or turn off negative ones. The emotions that motivate us to learn, to thrive, to push ourselves to succeed, or to engage with others are not just positive ones. We are also motivated, and even driven by, negative emotions. Negative emotions motivate us to avoid experiences that trigger them, or they urge us to behave in ways that will relieve their effects (Tomkins, 2008). For example, we may distract ourselves away from something that may activate sadness. If we do become sad when we remember something endearing about a loved one who died (in this case, perhaps lonely, empty, or sorrowful), we are motivated to do something that will help us feel better. What we decide to do in this regard may be healthy or unhealthy; for example, we might go for a walk in the woods, or we might consume alcohol to the point of intoxication. Our emotional expressions are a form of communication that display to others what we feel. The facial expression associated with sadness signals a need for comfort and may allow others to become aware of that need, and perhaps provide relief through comforting words, a hot cup of tea, or an invitation to dinner (Ekman, 2003).

Grief-Related Emotional Experiences

Emotions are immediate, reflexive responses to a specific stimulus, such as a situation, an image, or a thought. When an emotion instantaneously illuminates a memory, we find ourselves wondering why we are suddenly thinking about a particular person or reliving an event in our mind. Loss-related emotions may be experienced as continuous, intermittent, or activated suddenly and for no apparent reason.

> At times, the continuity of emotions and related thoughts may seem oppressive or exhausting.

When emotions are *continuous*, a particular process occurs whereby thoughts and emotions repeatedly reactivate one another. Thoughts can trigger emotion just as emotion motivates thoughts and images (Lerner & Keltner, 2000). This circularity of thought and emotion is familiar to people who have recently experienced a significant loss. At times, the continuity of emotions and related thoughts may seem oppressive or exhausting. For example, after her husband's death, Susan became preoccupied with whether or not she should move to a new house or perhaps an entirely new city. A continuous activation of distress can result from living in a home that was shared with a deceased loved one, and the surviving partner may believe they have to immediately change their physical environment.

Susan instead remodeled the rooms of her home, which contained prominent reminders of her husband. Her emotions were repeatedly triggered by his mementos, books, and favorite chair, which continuously led to thoughts of missing him. After reading literature that suggested surrounding yourself with reminders of lost loved ones, Susan wondered, momentarily, if she was wrong to change her living environment. "He knows I love him," she explained. "I don't want to wallow in my grief. I don't want to keep reliving my past life. I want to live my life now." For Susan, then, remodeling her environment provided some relief and inhibited her inclination to sell their home.

A narrative written by a grieving reader of my blog speaks to the continuous activation of emotions and thoughts, and to the possibility of resolution:

> My mother died about 5 weeks ago. I moved in with her last summer because I thought I could help her and enjoy some time with her. Then we found out she was sick, and I was the caregiver. Now I feel so alone, with her stuff all over the house. I get confused as to how much I want to clean things out and make it more me. I get confused when I drive by a street name that I knew would remind me of her after she died, knowing that I'd drive by it after she was gone. I used to wonder how I would feel to see it. I keep hoping that one day, going to work, I'll pass by that street sign, and smile a bit instead of looking at it like [it is] a monster. The grief is still a bit overwhelming.

Certain situations, events, images, or thoughts will activate loss-related emotions because situations we experience in the present provide a template or pattern-matching for memory traces that involved a deceased loved one. A specific date, such as the anniversary of a loss, may trigger an emotion. Mariella explained that for 2 weeks she had been sad and moody for no reason. Her body felt heavy and tired, and she found herself unnecessarily picking on the nice person she had been dating. She added, "Maybe it's because I don't deserve to date a nice guy." When asked if the particular week, month, or time of year had any significance to her, she suddenly realized that her feelings corresponded with the date of her late husband's cancer diagnosis, which had led to his death months later.

> The sudden activation of emotion may occur when memory traces are triggered by something that is not within our conscious awareness.

The sudden activation of emotion may occur when memory traces are triggered by something that is not within our conscious awareness, similar to what Kevin experienced as he settled into his seat in the theater, or Mariella's "mysterious" mood. Similarly, consciously remembering a situation that involves a loved one who has died can evoke feelings that range from mild sadness to anguish, like Susan felt when she saw her dead husband's possessions. Sensory information can ignite *emotional recall*, which is discussed in Chapter 6. Recalling the past, intentionally or unintentionally, can elicit an emotional response. Enjoyable or painful emotions may be activated by a memory, but we generally feel them less intensely than we did at the time of the original experience.

Emotional Memories and Scripts

Each time a particular emotion is triggered, we are pulled backward in time to experience some representation of a similar or related emotion (Nathanson, 1992). Along with remembrances of painful emotions are recollections of all the ways we have made ourselves feel better when we hurt (Nathanson, 1992). Every one of us has a library of coping responses to deal with painful emotional experiences. These coping mechanisms may include those we develop from early losses in our lives; however, they may not prepare us for the death of someone we love later in our lives; instead, they may compound the loss.

In other words, the emotions we experience in the present have histories. These *emotional memories* become compressed into mini-theories that automatically help us make sense of patterns and changes in our lives and provide information concerning ways of living in the world (Tomkins, 1995). Therefore, our *narrative scripts* involve emotional experiences to which we have assigned meaning and in reaction to which we have developed learned responses or scripted behaviors (Singer, 2004). The culture and environment in which we were raised may encourage particular emotional expressions and may discourage others. For example, if the existence of certain feelings—such as anger or sadness—was denied, we may have trouble perceiving and understanding a particular emotion (Tomkins, 1995). Likewise, if the expression of grief was deemed publicly unacceptable, we may suppress it. Given the scripting of our emotions, the emotional recall of an early loss that is triggered by a present loss likely is what led theorists to speculate that people who have suffered from an early loss or abandonment also experience prolonged or complicated grief (what Freud, 1917, referred to as "melancholia"; see also Chapter 3 of this book).

THE UNIQUE ROLE OF SHAME IN GRIEF

One of the negative emotions—shame—is designed to alert us when positive feeling states are temporarily blocked or disrupted. For example, as a young adolescent I was excited to go to school and see my friends, but if one of them mentioned my dead mother, my good feelings were impeded, and I temporarily withdrew. I would eventually reconnect. It is interesting how shame alerts us to a sense of disconnection from others and motivates us to restore the good feelings we have lost. In my case, shame alerted me, I momentarily withdrew, then I attempted to distract myself and my friends away from the idea that I was sad, and we were able to find happier footing.

> **The way shame operates in grief has a lot to do with why we are motivated to continue our bonds with loved ones who have died.**

People typically think of shame only in terms of how it makes us believe that our entire self is bad. We feel disconnected from our positive feelings. However, a primary—and helpful—role of shame is to inform us when an interpersonal bond has broken (Kaufman, 1974). When my mother told me she was "going to heaven," the sense of abandonment I felt made me want to hide. I now recognize that I was experiencing the shame of disconnection. Unfortunately, as is the case in all losses, restoring the good feelings that disappeared when I lost my mother was impossible. However, shame motivated me and allowed me to restore my connection to her and the consequent good feelings by creating an ongoing inner relationship with my mother. It is interesting to note that the way shame operates in grief has a lot to do with why we are motivated to continue our bonds with lost loved ones, a topic I touch on later in this chapter.

Childhood loss may influence a later response to loss in adulthood. In some situations, a romantic partner may serve as an anesthetic of sorts, or a coping device to manage earlier experiences of loss-related shame and a sense of unworthiness (Dellmann, 2018). When a partner dies, the survivor's hidden early shame experience may result in a prolonged grief response. For example, the death of

Susan's husband brought forth feelings she had not experienced since her mother had abandoned her as an 8-year-old child. Early in her life, Susan's emotions had become scripted, enabling her to avoid attachments that might lead to the anguish of loss. Recalling many years of dating people she did not love, Susan said she had been conscious of not wanting to risk feeling the pain of desertion. At nearly 50 years old, she met Evan, who became the love of her life, despite her initial efforts to shun him. She recalled, "It was the first time in my life I let someone love me and allowed myself to love them, too." When Evan tragically died, she emotionally reexperienced the abandonment she had felt as a child. On a cognitive level, Susan recognized that Evan did not intentionally abandon her as her mother had done. However, she *felt* as though it were the same. If we understand the notion of scripted emotional responses, we can learn from them and even modify our responses. However, they also can hinder us as we interpret, evaluate, and make predictions on the basis of our experiences. In Susan's case, when she recognized that Evan's death triggered emotional memories of being abandoned by her mother, she better understood her past experience of loss and was able to observe how it influenced her responses in the present.

> **We do not have to justify our grieving experience.**

Shame sensitivity to grief is often based on an early loss experience when exposing vulnerability to others resulted in shame. For example, when a child cries in class and is taunted for being a crybaby, this can make it pretty hard to show sadness. A variant of shame is experienced by adults who believe grief is a sign of weakness, isolating themselves for fear of risking humiliation for expressing what they feel (Dellmann, 2018). Moreover, we may experience shame if we encounter people who dismiss how we feel or make disparaging remarks about our grief experiences. One of the readers of my blog wrote the following:

> It's surprising to me how many people in my life refused to let me grieve properly. It started early on. They said things to me like "He's gone!" "Just move on!" "You're enabling yourself to feel sad." I even remember being called rude because I cried the day of his memorial after I got home and read the condolence cards. "You read those cards knowing it would make you sad!" my sister-in-law screamed (as if I'd committed some horrible crime).

How can we respond to those who do not understand what we feel, urge us to move on, or convey other shaming messages? It is important to know that we can own how we feel. Another person can say anything they choose, but nobody *makes* us feel ashamed. We experience shame in such encounters because we believe something is wrong with us, or we assume we have something to be ashamed about. It is imperative to accept what we feel even if we believe others cannot understand it or cannot tolerate what they feel when they are exposed to our grief. We do not have to convince anyone what our own experience should be. Grief is unique to each person who encounters it.

Throughout my years of practice, many clients who continue to privately mourn the loss of a loved one have hesitantly shared their concern that something is wrong with them. Why would something be wrong with us for missing someone who seems, or perhaps is, irreplaceable? People are not interchangeable. Anyone whose child, close sibling, or soul mate has died clearly knows that nothing can replace what they have lost. The rest of our life continues to go on, but grief-related memories rest in our minds, poised to arise with any trigger. Thus, if we are not ashamed of what we feel, we can respond more easily to someone who does not understand. We may not be able to help others understand something they have not encountered, but we may be able to elicit empathy and support.

People who mourn may actually be fortunate that their love for another person remains alive with them, even though at times it hurts. Loss hurts because we have invested our love in someone who no longer exists, except within us. Eventually we accept that our loved one exists only in our static memories—they do not experience the present along with us, except in our minds. Thus, we adjust our narratives about who we are without them in the reality of our lives, even though they may continue to be with us as we once knew them. Repetitive experiences whereby our hopes are met with limits result in grief. For example, my husband loved the hummingbirds that lived in our trees and bathed in our fountain. When I saw a tiny baby hummingbird I felt inclined to call out to him to see it. I felt him near, but sadly I also knew that I was sharing my joy only with his image as it exists within me. The distress and shame of disconnection require hope that our positive emotions will return. When that hope is gone, we experience some other negative emotion, in this case, grief or anguish.

Shame and Bereavement-Related Depression

The role of shame is often overlooked or neglected in treating bereavement-related depression, yet shame is a prominent component in depressive syndromes and is considered by some theorists as central in the experience of depression (H. B. Lewis, 1987; Morrison, 1987; Wurmser, 2015). As described earlier in this chapter, when something disrupts our positive emotions, shame is activated (Tomkins, 2008). Therefore, one way to describe depression is as a syndrome of distress and shame, whereby emotion and memory produce a continuous experience of negative feelings (Nathanson, 1992; Tomkins, 2008).

Some researchers have speculated that shame experiences in interpersonal contexts activate maladaptive cognitive–affective spirals that result in depression (Thompson & Berenbaum, 2006). In other words, shame can worsen depression, and it can compound itself. Grievers may interpret the sense of sadness and defeat related to a shame-based depression as a personal inadequacy (Tomkins, 2008). Thus, when grieving individuals are told they just have to "get over it," they are further shamed. I discuss depression in more detail later in this chapter.

Shame and Sense of Self

Emotion theorists who have associated the sense of disconnection, indignity, self-consciousness, and alienation with the emotion of shame emphasize that the way we and others perceive the self makes a difference (H. B. Lewis, 1971; Nathanson, 1992; Tomkins, 2008). Our experience of ourselves changes as a consequence of shame in that shame shakes one's self-esteem and self-respect (Czub, 2013). We feel shame as a sickness of the soul or as an inner torment, and it makes us feel defeated, alienated, and lacking in dignity or worth (Tomkins, 2008). An inability to express inner pain and need also separates one from the rest of humanity (Kaufman, 1974). Therefore, within the shadows of loss-related memories may lurk the shame of disconnection and its influence on one's sense of self. It is important to be alert to this. The shame of disconnection may lead us to attack ourselves or others, withdraw, or use avoidance as a coping strategy. My own struggle with the shame of loss and disconnection as well as the longing that accompanied it became part of my story, as did my eventual ability to learn from it, which is an adaptive response to shame. Thus, if we find ourselves responding to disconnection by withdrawing; through avoidance maneuvers such excessive drinking, shopping, or indulging ourselves in some way; or by attacking ourselves or others, then we know it is time to sit with the distress of disconnection and accept what we can learn from our feelings. Shame and distress associated with disconnection from a loved one often result in a longing for reconnection. Writing down our feelings and the responses we have to them provides an opportunity to engage in inner exploration and learning.

DISTRESS AND LONGING

In Portuguese and Galician languages, the word "saudade" refers to the presence of an absence, an "intimate feeling and mood caused by the longing for something absent that is being missed" ("Saudade," 2021). Saudade is familiar to bereft individuals even if the word is not in their vocabulary. Such grief is different from that of everyday sadness. Separation from someone we love may lead us to experience distress or its more intense version, anguish. Like all negative emotions, distress motivates us to do something that will relieve its effects. In situations involving separation, we experience sensations of distress as yearning and a longing for reconnection. When a loved one has died, the survivor's distress may motivate one to seek a reunion despite the impossibility of achieving that goal. Happily, though, we can do something to help restore a broken bond, relieving ourselves from the effects of separation distress. For example, in everyday life with a partner, people are inclined to make up after a disagreement. Separation distress that motivates people to hang onto a failing relationship is harmful, but when it leads one to open oneself to new, if different, relationships, it is helpful.

Emotional memories play a significant role in the formation of personality and in how we adjust to life experiences, including loss. Memories regulate our emotions and our satisfaction with our lives (Wilson & Ross, 2003); however, loss may leave us rather helpless to control the valence of our emotions, so when we have lost a loved one we often experience mixed emotional states.

Mixed Emotions, Longing, and Bittersweet Memories

We tend to believe that recalling a pleasant personal experience will improve a bad mood and that remembering a distressing personal episode will worsen it; however, a contrast effect may also occur (Wilson & Ross, 2003). Merely recalling a happy memory of someone who has died may activate sadness that reminds us of their loss. For example, Jessica explained that, after her mother died, mundane positive situations would trigger a profound negative emotional response in her. In one instance, she ordered school pictures for her children and realized she could now purchase fewer because her mother wouldn't need any. These situations, Jessica noted, "seem to come out of nowhere and catch me completely off guard. They feel like an emotional tsunami that turns me into a human puddle. It is humbling to go through this, especially in a public place."

> **Merely recalling a happy memory of someone who has died may activate sadness that reminds us of their loss.**

The emotions we experience in recalling enjoyable moments with a loved one may vacillate rapidly between positive and negative, as when we feel the distress of their loss. In situations of loss, the recall of a positive emotional memory is often followed by the rapid triggering of a negative emotion. We automatically reappraise the situation in light of our present circumstances. As a result, we experience nostalgia and bittersweetness, which researchers refer to as "ambivalent affect" (Vaccaro et al., 2020). A similar mixed positive

75

and negative state was found in addiction cravings (Veilleux et al., 2013). Ambivalent affect is a universal experience, although such feelings are described differently across individuals, cultures, and contexts (Vaccaro et al., 2020). Researchers who have studied the concept of love among people in the United States, Italy, and China found that it has both similar and different meanings cross-culturally. There are synonyms for "love" in the English language, but only Chinese includes "sad love" and "sorrow love" (Rothbaum & Tsang, 1998).

I think of love not as an emotion but more a condition that can embody an emotional state or mood. Love involves a mixture of emotions, such as excitement or joy, that leads to happiness or sensory pleasure. Along with shame, sadness is a painful state of disconnection from someone or something that we value. Profound sadness or sad love, as it relates to traditional concepts of love, can be triggered by an observation, event, or acknowledgment that the object of your affection is inaccessible. Unrequited affection also causes sadness. People who experience the death of a beloved describe sadness as a ghost of the good things they shared with another person. Beautiful memories, not ugly ones, trigger what we might describe as sad love. Through vivid emotional memories, our sad love tightly clings to what has been lost. Because we cannot erase our memories, someone or something may always activate them, if intermittently.

> **We may find comfort in focusing our attention on what we had, rather than on our yearning to restore what is impossible to replicate in the present.**

Under circumstances of grief, what are we likely to do with what we feel? Over time, we acquire a capacity to tolerate loss-related feelings. Although memories may be bittersweet, we may find comfort in focusing our attention on what we had rather than on our yearning to restore what is impossible to replicate in the present. Recognizing that our distress motivates us to search for what we lost, we may be somewhat relieved if we can revel in the enjoyment we once experienced. In this regard, the Japanese word "natsukashii" refers to a nostalgic longing, but one that includes joy and gratitude for the past rather than a desire to return to it. Nevertheless, the initial emotion activated by reminders of a loved one often motivate us to seek a reunion with them.

Searching

After the loss of her husband, Erica became concerned that her memory was becoming impaired, and she was embarrassed to reveal the mental lapses. On a daily basis she was unable to find things like her sunglasses or watch. Certain that she had misplaced whatever she was trying to find, she would search the house. She eventually would find what she had been looking for, which was exactly where she had expected the item to be in the first place, but she had not seen it. She explained. "Eventually I realized, in a metaphorical sense, I was always looking for my husband."

In the initial weeks, and sometimes months, after the death of a loved one, people commonly experience "losing something" or having instances of searching for something thought to be lost. Some of my clients who have discussed the death of a significant person in their lives have reported losing things important to them, such as car keys or documents, that later are found in plain view. They have described entering a room to find something and then forgetting what they are seeking. In some cases, they "see" something they do not realize they are seeking, that is, their lost loved one in a car on the road, walking in the distance, or in a dream.

For example, after my husband's death, I kept finding myself searching for things that were right before my eyes that I could not see, such as scissors, a tape measure, or my phone. Eventually, I became amused by my own distraction and the inclination of my memory to tell me something was missing when in fact it was in plain sight. But I wasn't the only one who seemed to be searching. My older son's little dog, who was particularly fond of my husband and would always howl upon seeing him, seemed to be searching as well. When my son visited, his dog would dart through our home and then stand paralyzed in our hallway as though he were waiting for his good friend, my husband, to appear.

We often meld grief and the search for a lost loved one. The search for lost things is a common literary theme that includes the quest for reunification, the effort to find one's way home, or the discovery of the place where lost treasures go. The theme has also been used to depict a safe place, such as in the poet Rainer Maria Rilke's writing of sheltering his soul "among remote lost objects, in some dark and silent place" (Rilke, 1907/1995). "The Place Where Lost Things Go" is a soothing song for children about the loss of their mother that was written for the 2018 movie *Mary Poppins Returns*. The lyrics reassure the children that their mother is "smiling from a star that she makes glow" and they can find her in the place "where the lost things go" (Blunt, 2018).[2]

The patron saint of lost things is St. Anthony, who was born Fernando Martins de Bulhoes in the year 1195. The tradition of praying to St. Anthony for lost or stolen things is said to have originated from an incident in Bologna, Italy, where he lost an important

---

[2]"The Place Where Lost Things Go" was written by Marc Shaiman and Scott Whitman for the Walt Disney film *Mary Poppins Returns*, which was directed by Rob Marshall.

book of psalms that contained his teaching notes (Perry, 2000). Because, in those days, such books were difficult if not impossible to replace, he prayed that it would be found or returned. According to the legend, the thief (a novice who had grown tired of religious life and had left the order) was so moved that he returned the book and reunited with the order. St. Anthony, among other saints, is also the patron saint of fishermen and sailors, along with travelers and vacationers, who often pray to him for their safety. Although I recognized that St. Anthony, my father's namesake, would not bring back my husband, I came across a medallion of St. Anthony in my husband's belongings that I had given him, and carried it around in my pocket during the weeks after his loss.

Distress is alleviated by a reunion, as we know when we find lost keys, put our hands on a misplaced document, or discover that a friend still loves us despite whatever stupid thing we may have done. The emotionally motivating responses essential to maintaining a relationship when the loved one is alive—such as keeping in close touch—continue to operate when the loved one has died (Archer, 1999). Now, though, we may experience the motivation for a reconnection, and any hopelessness associated with its futility, as grief.

Separation distress and shame associated with grief can become anguishing simply because they motivate us to reconnect or to repair a broken bond when it is not feasible, or even possible. We may long for reunification, but what about when someone is forever lost and will never be found again in our lifetime? Some theorists believe the seeking impulse, as a response to death, is a painful, and perhaps even a maladaptive, response (Archer, 1999). Thus, in grief, we must psychically reorganize, dealing with the *absence* of the emotional connection with the lost loved one. Although replacing someone with whom we have a deep emotional attachment is not easily accomplished—and, in some cases, impossible—some people find a creative solution through the use of imagery, which is discussed in Chapter 5.

DEPRESSION AND ANGER TURNED AGAINST THE SELF

When we say someone "suffers" from depression, we imagine a level of unhappiness ranging from sorrow to deep despair. Depression arises from a particular event, circumstance, or situation that activates continuous distress or anguish. Emotions always make us pay attention to whatever triggers them, and in the case of separation distress we usually focus on reminders of the person to whom we are strongly attached; that is, our attention becomes biased.[3]

When depression turns our attention inward, distress gets magnified. However, an inward turning of attention may also promote resignation and, in a more positive vein, acceptance (Izard, 1977). Depression can be thought of as a harbinger of change. It can provide an opportunity to consider revising our objectives and strategies for the future, especially if we want to escape the depression (Henretty et al., 2008). This is a very internal process, though, and when others imply that we can simply overcome depression we may find we just feel distressed or ashamed to be suffering from the condition. It is important to be mindful of all the possibilities.

Loss-related depression has been misunderstood for decades. A mainstay since the Freudian era is the notion that depression represents anger directed toward the self or turned inward. This view assumes that anger is directed toward the self in the form of self-attack, rather than toward the person who has died. Such thinking is based on the notion that early childhood loss results in the child's ambivalent feelings toward the lost parent and then later leads to a vulnerability to self-directed anger whenever we encounter loss. Cognitive behavior therapy, especially in its earliest incarnation, also

---

[3]Attentional and emotional symptoms of separation distress were found to result from variation in brain activity and connectivity associated with the amygdala, the region where emotional processing occurs (Freed et al., 2009).

linked depression with anger turned against the self; this was said to account for the blame, criticism, disgust, and hatred that people who are depressed direct against themselves (A. T. Beck, 1964, 1972).

Many symptoms of depression directly involve coping responses to shame. These include withdrawal (e.g., hypersomnia, not wanting to be in the presence of others or engage in activities), avoidance (e.g., drug and alcohol abuse), attack-other behaviors (e.g., irritability/ raging at others, or blaming others for causing the negative mood), and attack-self responses (e.g., self-injurious behaviors and suicide attempts; Nathanson, 1992). The attack-self coping response to shame is particularly prominent in depression. When persistent shame and enduring fear arise in close proximity, they are likely to be experienced as anger that is turned against the self.

> **In loss-related circumstances we tend to remember positive experiences and put aside our disappointments.**

For the most part, people recognize when they are angry at a loved one, even though they may not understand the actual source of the anger. This dynamic may shift when the person we love has died. First of all, under such circumstances we tend to remember positive experiences and put aside our disappointments. Eventually, we can accept some of our less positive thoughts and feelings, and it is important that we allow ourselves to do so. For example, the first Christmas season after her husband's death, Shannon experienced a tremendous fear of loneliness. The thought of being without him on a holiday was horribly distressing. She stepped back from her feelings, recollecting that her husband did not like the holidays and that he had agreed to only minimally celebrate them. He had refused to attend gatherings with family members or friends, and over their many years together she had reluctantly conceded. Shannon then reached out to her husband's relatives, whose holiday invitations had always been turned down. They enthusiastically invited her to join them. The celebration, in her estimation, was the best she had experienced in her life, and she left feeling joyful and loved. Upon arriving home, Shannon picked up the photograph of her husband, as she often did upon entering the house. She kissed his image and said, "You shit; I love you, but you are so selfish."

REMEMBERING, FORGETTING, AND RESPONSE TO TRAUMA

Is it better to try to recall traumatic emotional memories of loss or to attempt to block them out of one's mind? In the past, therapists have assigned value to recalling trauma in pursuit of a fuller integration of the inner experiences that result from it. Recalling traumatic memories may be at odds with an individual's need to reduce emotional responses by suppressing intrusive memories (Gagnepain et al., 2017), yet the capacity to push unpleasant past experiences out of one's mind may not be easily controlled by willpower or by directed thinking and feeling activities, such as "trying to forget it" (M. C. Anderson & Levy, 2009). Such commonsense suppressions leave the memory and negative emotion within the range of our awareness, so the self-reflexive activation of memory may continue, if not become stronger (M. C. Anderson & Levy, 2009).

When a grieving person aches for their lost connection with a loved one, items such as the dead person's belongings evoke memories that create a soothing presence within the absence. On the other hand, anything that continually triggers emotional memories of a longed-for person who has died may extend loss-related emotions and amplify grief. When we are trying to decide whether to keep reminders of the deceased in our living spaces we must assess whether the objects provide comfort or activate distress. This is a deeply personal decision. Perhaps a middle ground can be achieved by putting the items aside until enough time has passed so that a grief response upon seeing them one is not so intense.

Trauma and Triggers

People who have experienced interpersonal trauma may unfortunately seek out or engage in self-triggering reminders of their traumatic events (Bellet, Jones, et al., 2020). This triggering may result from perceiving that the trauma is central to one's identity. But the trauma can become, as a result, more significant to one's identity if the repetition gives it a prominent role. People may be motivated to self-trigger in an attempt to make meaning of the traumatic event, or to control or predict how they feel, such as when they make efforts to match an internal state of distress with an external experience (Bellet, Jones, et al., 2020). For example, writing the following personal narrative was self-triggering for me, but only mildly so at this point in my life. I considered completely eliminating it from this book, given I did not want to activate these memories. In adulthood, for the most part, I put aside the emotions I had felt as an adolescent in relation to my abusive stepmother and my father's inability to protect his children. However, this followed several years of psychotherapy and a course of psychoanalysis during my own training as an analyst. Even in psychotherapy, though, I did not often focus on my stepmother's erratic and vitriolic behavior. Immersed in my education and job, I was future focused, motivated to live beyond my past. Nevertheless, when we write or think about an adverse experience in our lives, it sends us down memory lane to places we'd rather not visit. So, as I wrote what follows, there were moments when I refused to engage with the fleeting imagery created by particular memories that were activated. Granted, they may emerge later in dreams or when I least expect them, but I know I am distant from them and that they won't hurt me.

After my father's death, I visited my stepmother only once, nearly a decade later and only for 15 minutes. Prior to that time, we had occasionally corresponded through cordial letters that contained little substance. I doubt that arranging this isolated self-triggering visit was an attempt to make meaning of my adolescent experiences with my stepmother. More likely it was motivated by missing my father and my inclination to do the right thing based on my loyalty to him and his values. In this case, "the right thing" was to introduce her to my child, who at the time was less than 1 year old.

My stepmother lived in a modern trailer, yet the untidy, disheveled interior of her dwelling reflected unkempt habits I remembered of her from my youth, and they were quite opposite to my mother's standards. I found a place to sit, next to a coffee table piled high with miscellaneous things, and within minutes my son squirmed off my lap, wanting to stand while supporting himself by holding the edge of the table. He reached for a pair of scissors that lay in the pile of other items, and as I moved them out of his reach, my stepmother said sharply, "No! Bad boy, bad boy."

I felt sensations of distress and sadness. Rather than ignore them in the same way my father had ignored the abuse, I lifted my child into my arms, politely said it was time for us to go, and immediately headed for the door. On the way, I noticed pencils scattered on the counter and was reminded of how she had stabbed me, unexpectedly, with newly sharpened pencils, leaving "tattoos" of lead in my arms and back. But that was the least of it. I interrupted the flood of memories by focusing on my child. On the drive home, as I passed the cemetery where my father was buried, through silent thoughts I let him know that I could no longer be his little soldier. Several years later, I was informed of my stepmother's death, but I did not attend the funeral.

Losing someone who was cruel or abusive does not necessarily bring with it a sense of relief or liberation from the person—unless, of course, we remained in contact with the abuser, or the abuse had been continuous until their death (Elison & McGonigle, 2003). The limited research that has examined the emotional impact of an abusive perpetrator's death on the victim points out that complications in the victim's grieving process can arise; these stem from the victim's experience of conflicting or ambivalent emotions (Lin et al., 2021; Monahan, 2003). For example, a study of women who were child sex abuse survivors found that the death of their abusers resulted in grief that reflected a complex relationship with the abuser. Themes in the women's narratives included the perception of the funeral as a liability rather than a benefit and that the death represented a loss of the opportunity for confrontation or clarity (Lin et al., 2021; Monahan, 2003). Women also regretted that others failed to understand their multilayered grief. We cannot generalize the impact of abuse on the bereavement process, however, because both grief and abuse are highly personal experiences. The death of an abuser adds further complexity to bereavement given that it involves myriad possibilities regarding the nature of the abuse, how the abuse was handled, and many other circumstances.

Research supports the notion that responses to trauma are more maladaptive when the central focus is on the negative outcomes of the event instead of on centralizing the event positively by attempting to work through the experience and finding meaning in it (Broadbridge, 2018). In other words, the cognitive mastery of trauma, according to some researchers, represents attempts by victims to generate a theory of the traumatic event and create meaning from it (Kauffman, 2002a). For many people, however, the notion of finding meaning in the trauma experience or focusing on positive aspects may seem ludicrous. Some people may lament that they have been told to focus on the positive when they find little that is optimistic about their experience of trauma, and this urging by others can even lead them to believe the problem lies within them. Moreover, as some studies have shown, blame and self-blame can involve attempts to generate a theory of an event and seek a means of control about what one feels (Kauffman, 2002a).

Responses to loss and trauma vary among people, of course. Much of our understanding about how people respond to a traumatic event or loss is derived from those who have struggled with the aftermath and seek help from psychotherapists to better cope with their memories and emotions. According to researchers, some individuals demonstrate resilience and an ability to maintain a stable equilibrium in response to trauma and loss, in contrast to those who seek to recover from an experience (Bonanno, 2004). Nevertheless, the grief of resilient individuals is not absent. Many people characterized as resilient experience yearning and emotional pangs, and early after loss they report episodes of rumination and intrusive thoughts (Bonanno, 2004).

There are times when we may have to revisit an emotionally distressing memory before we can suppress or control it (Depue et al., 2007). In essence, it is vital to recognize what we feel at a given moment and understand how this corresponds to the imagery and thoughts associated with painful memories. This helps us find ways to inhibit or distract ourselves and to control the urge to revisit the past through thoughts that only disturb us. Thus, by suppressing the sensory aspects of memory (especially given that traumatic events are initially recalled in a sensory form), and through repeated practice strengthening cognitive control over one's recollections, memories can be somewhat controlled (Depue et al., 2007).

Although we don't "get over" a trauma or loss, the experiences associated with one are subject to the fate of all of our memories. In other words, if we do not constantly replay memories in our minds, they seem to fade beneath the layers of all the memories that follow, unless some sort of retrieval cue prompts their recall. In this sense, the passage of time can provide a resting place for grief- and trauma-related memories. This subject is explored further in Chapter 7.

Strain Trauma and Loss

Long-lasting situations that create an accumulation of frustrating tensions—such as caring for a dying loved one—may cause traumatic effects known as *strain trauma* (Kris, 1956; Weiss, 1993). Prolonged states of emotional distress, physical tension, and cognitive preoccupation with the long-term suffering or deterioration of someone who is dying can affect a caregiver's physical health, relationships, career, and sense of self. Moreover, memories of caring for a terminally ill loved one can later become coupled with the effects of their loss.

> **What we experience as we bear witness to death may seem inexpressible.**

Throughout my years of practice, many clients have noted that as children they experienced a parent's terminal illness. Expressed merely as a fact, left unsaid is that significant emotional experience and intrusive memories resulted from witnessing a parent's decline and death. Similarly, adults who observe the progressive decline and death of a child, partner, sibling, friend, or parent also state the fact of the matter, relaying the information while leaving out the emotional impact. Why is this? Because what we experience as we bear witness to death may seem inexpressible. Indeed, this was true as I watched my own mother slowly deteriorate. I watched her decreasing awareness of the outside world; I saw her eventually become unable to speak, or eat, or drink. I had no words for the assaults to my sense of self; it was all I could do to simply express the fact that as a child I had watched my mother die—if I dared to reveal that information at all.

I have repeatedly mentioned that grief is a very personal emotional experience. Cognitively, it is private as well. Philosopher Rupert Read (2018) explained the double bind of grief: In our loneliness we desperately want to be accepted, yet we may find ourselves wanting what we are going through *not* to be understandable by others. We want it to be ours and ours alone. Experiences of loss and grief, he believed, may be cognitively closed to others. How we cognitively remember loss is the subject of the next chapter.

TO SUMMARIZE

The concept of emotional memory describes the effects of emotion on episodic memory and refers to a consciously remembered experience that activates an emotional reaction. Emotions and emotional experiences become scripted throughout our lives and may be implicated in prolonged grief responses. Classification systems of emotions describe primary, or core emotions. The emotional states of anxiety, longing, depression, love, or grief result from the blending of primary emotions. Some of our negative emotions are designed to impede or disrupt positive feeling states.

The notion of depression as representing anger directed toward the self or turned inward may neglect the role of shame. Depression is best described as a syndrome of distress/anguish and shame, whereby emotion and memory produce continuous negative feelings. In grief, our emotions are subject to contrast effects and unusual behaviors that represent separation distress.

The process of adapting to and coping with loss is a subjective emotional experience; however, the emotions experienced by a grieving person can be confusing because they are often accompanied by thoughts that reflect impossible motives. Loss-related emotions may be experienced as continuous or intermittent, and they may be activated suddenly.

Reflections

- Think about the way you cope with painful emotions (e.g., how do you make yourself feel better when you are hurting?). If your coping methods involve withdrawal, avoidance, attacking yourself, or attacking/ blaming others, consider whether they have helped or hurt you, and how you might respond differently.
- Expressions of grief may be overt and spontaneous, or they may be hidden. Do you hide your feelings from others, or are you transparent with what you feel? What responses do you receive from others? Do they ask about how you feel? If you hide your grief, do they collude in ignoring it?
- Do the objects that remind you of a loved one who has died provide comfort, or do they activate distress/anguish? What decisions have you made about putting those items aside or keeping them in your sight, and what emotions motivated your choices?
- What thoughts and behaviors "self-trigger" your emotional responses to loss? Do you find yourself repetitively activating emotional memories that are painful?

CHAPTER 5

GRIEF THOUGHTS

The new seventh-grade books stacked on my bedroom desk were joyless. After my mother died, I became keenly aware that something was wrong with my ability to concentrate, memorize information, and recall facts. Every mediocre test score was humiliating. I assumed my former abilities existed only because my mother had been there to drill me on spelling words, correct my little essays, and prepare me for history tests. I concluded that I wasn't very smart after all.

According to British philosopher Rupert Read (2018), the logic of profound grief is peculiar and hard to understand, even for its sufferer. As the travel companion of emotion, cognition uses the logic of thought to inform what we feel. We instantaneously apply to present experiences what we have learned or have come to understand from similar past experiences, and we tuck away in our memory how we have made sense of emotion, so that we may summon this knowledge for the future when we experience loss or pain anew.

The logic of profound grief remains mysterious, in part because it is as unique as the life stories from which it emerges. For the past 100 years, serious thinkers have attempted to make sense of grief, applying various theoretical frameworks that might give it a recognizable face. But it may be that only in the context of a deeply personal history that grief can be logical.

In the early periods of grieving, and sometimes beyond, thinking may become cloudy, and emotional responses may seem unusual. Ordinarily, autobiographical remembering helps to protect our sense of self when we must cope with adverse circumstances that activate intense emotion or threaten to destabilize our self-concept (Pasupathi, 2003; Robinson, 1986; Ross & Wilson, 2003). Strangely, in moments of grief, these cognitive and emotional processes that usually ensure stability may seem to function inadequately.

The notion that we process grief has been a mainstay in our culture; however, many grief-related experiences are challenging, if not impossible, to process. Actual information processing involves cognition: thinking about something that has happened to us, using thought to make sense of what is felt, and assigning meaning to it. But the thoughts accompanying our emotional responses to loss may result in intrusive imagery, ruminations, or concentration difficulties that do not seem to make sense. Thus, when we lose someone we love, we may be unable to use thought to make sense of what we feel. On the other hand, we may deliberately attempt to find meaning in a loss to mute painful emotion and changes within us. Finally, cognition enables us to form conscious mental images of the deceased, or unconscious images that are represented overtly in imagery or symbolically in dreams. Indeed, our current experiences are integrated with memories of the deceased as we sleep.

At first glance, some of the things people say, do, or believe in response to a significant loss may seem illogical. Many people privately continue a relationship with the departed, communicating through fantasies, prayers, rituals, and/or conversations, or through the belief that the deceased person is with them on certain marker days (e.g., a wedding anniversary). Others make sense of loss by blaming themselves, blaming someone else, or imagining that their fate resulted from something completely unfounded. Some individuals create meaning from the ashes of their losses. Meaning making can provide a justification for, or a greater purpose regarding, the loss. Alternatively, a loss may revise our self-perceptions in ways that lead us to seek personal meaningful experiences. In any case, how we think and what we believe are essential to our personal understanding of loss, grief, and the subsequent meanings we link to the experience. In this chapter, I attempt to make logical sense of the cognitive processes involved in grief-related experiences.

COGNITION

We use our cognitive abilities whenever we consciously think, remember, reason, or know. Cognition involves many aspects of mental functioning, including perception, attention, memory, imagery, language, reasoning, and decision making. Information acquired from living in the world and interacting with the environment becomes represented within our mind, enabling our cognitive processes to operate on these representations (McBride & Cutting, 2016). In other words, our cognitive abilities draw upon what we have learned in the past when we encounter similar situations in the present. Cognition means much more than thinking, however. Cognition transforms the general data of emotion, including signals and sensations from the body, into specifics that are based on thought processes.

In consciousness, cognition and emotion (thought and feeling) are travel companions, arising together to inform us. Although a person may be criticized for being either "too emotional" or "too much in their head," the fact is that cognition and emotion together contribute to how we function in the world. One is not necessarily privileged over the other, even though some of my colleagues might argue about the primacy of emotion or cognition. An emotion alerts us to something going on by magnifying whatever prompted it, providing sensory information and motivating our behavior. Cognition provides specific meaning to an emotion's general feeling by instantaneously searching through memories related to similar experiences and producing a thought. As a result, the thoughts we assign to feelings associated with loss involve a complex process within our brain.

Sadness, distress, or anguish of grief can disrupt our ability to think.

Some highly emotional events and stressful situations, such as having little time to get something done, can positively influence cognition, enabling us to become motivated, achieve better focus, and have greater accuracy in remembering information (Lamia, 2017). Other stressful influences, such as loss and mourning, may interfere with the fluency of our cognitions and the accuracy of our memories (McNally, 2003; Peace & Porter, 2004). The sadness, distress, or anguish of grief can disrupt our ability to think. These emotions demand immediate and focused attention on the source of what activated them, namely, loss. For example, when a partner dies, the surviving partner's changed situation may be financially, socially, or personally strenuous (Bowlby, 1980). Unlike generally stressful events, severe stress—such as an accident that leaves a partner on life support—can affect memory by altering our attention and interfering with what becomes encoded in memory and is available for later retrieval (Laney, 2013).

Our memory system needs time to adjust to changed circumstances.

We expect, on the basis of our past experiences, a certain predictability in many aspects of our lives. By forming schemata or *scripts*—memory templates—our memory system uses redundancies to prompt our expectations regarding events (Laney, 2013; Tomkins, 1995). The scripts that once provided us with information for a present circumstance may no longer apply in loss-related situations, however, even though our brain may attempt to apply them. Especially painful conditions occur when memory templates associated with positive feelings are impossible to replicate because the person involved is gone. The loss of a loved one leaves us dangling: We have a store of positive experiences that we cannot repeat in the future. We may know our loved one has died and is inaccessible, but our memory system needs time to adjust to changed circumstances. Moreover, joyful moments experienced together cannot be shared through reminiscence. For example, when my husband was alive, reminiscing with him about shared enjoyable past experiences was always pleasurable. After his death, however, recalling those same memories is bittersweet.

ATTENTION, CONCENTRATION, AND INTRUSIVE THOUGHTS

After the death of her long-term partner, Jaelyn was having difficulty falling asleep. When she went to bed, she actively tried to avoid thinking about him. Whenever she did not distract herself, she focused on her intense sadness and longing to see her partner again. Her strategy to avoid crying herself to sleep involved deliberately focusing her thoughts on her ex-husband. Any image of her ex-husband—"the cheating, lying rat"—disgusted and angered her. Unfortunately, those memories also kept her awake, but she assumed that was better than the anguish she felt about losing her partner.

Although Jaelyn's strategy did not help her fall asleep, her approach was not wholly incorrect. She was correct in that selectively attending to reminders of loss may maintain a person's agonizing mood and preoccupy them with the impossibility of reunion (Maccallum & Bryant, 2010). However, debilitating memories of loss are more easily triggered by negative emotions than by positive emotions (Maccallum & Bryant, 2010). Thus, Jaelyn may have been able to relax and fall asleep if she had focused on positive emotional memories concerning her deceased partner, such as how he had comforted or amused her, rather than on her anguish about missing him. Separating fond remembrances from the sadness of loss may be challenging; nevertheless, attempting to distinguish these as different experiences is essential to minimizing grief's anguish.

Sometimes we can control unwanted memories through voluntary suppression. When we want to dismiss something from our awareness, we may stop memory retrieval by using mechanisms similar to what we use to prevent a reflexive motor response, such as inhibiting a particular movement or action (M. C. Anderson & Levy, 2009). In many instances, inhibiting a body movement may be easier than stopping thoughts related to memory. We can attempt to interrupt a thought by saying to ourselves, "I'm not going to go there," or we can turn our attention away from the unwanted thoughts or whatever activated them by distracting ourselves. The more adept we become at suppressing painful memories, the better we can reduce our emotional responses to disturbing images and scenes (Gagnepain et al., 2017). You may also imagine that this line of thinking goes against the notion of expressing what we feel or delving into our grief and pain to process it. In many ways, and for a good reason, it does go against the grain of what we learn.

Sometimes the past should be left alone.

In my professional experience, I have found that sometimes the past should be left alone. Reliving the past and evaluating what we experienced can certainly clarify our judgment errors or any misrepresentation in our perception of a situation. Later in this chapter, we consider some of the regrets we experience after a loved one dies and how looking back can help us learn and gain perspective. Ruminating about a traumatic past or the things we regret, though, tends to stir up our emotional brain rather than calm it down. The more times we run down the same path, the more familiar, available, and accessible it may become.

If we can learn something from reviewing our past experiences, they are more likely to become neutralized and no longer so painful. Ruminating about them is different. Also, as we live our lives, many past unpleasant events become buried beneath new emotional memories, and these more recent memories can shield us from a painful past. We saw in Chapter 4 how Susan's marriage had buried her memories of abandonment; however, the death of her partner rekindled those old memories. Untangling our feelings around a current loss from memories of situations in the distant past may be difficult. A shared value in many psychotherapy approaches has to do with an interest in pursuing what we generally keep out of our conscious awareness, including exposure to painful memories. The therapist's value of fuller expression and integration of inner experiences may be at odds with a client's goal to effectively suppress painful thoughts and traumatic memories, including those related to loss (Berman, 2001).

When suicide is the cause of a loved one's death, the therapist's goal may be to provide comfort to help a client embrace a deep wound that cannot be analyzed out of existence rather than to uncover the traumatized survivor's painful memories (Balint, 1969). With this goal in mind, the individual can, it is hoped, discover their way into the world of others. We may, however, unexpectedly be reminded of a traumatic loss, as we saw in Chapter 4, when Kevin's memory of his father's suicide was triggered by similar circumstances surrounding the anniversary of his father's death. In these situations, we are remembering, but we are not in danger, and we will recover.

We cannot necessarily erase memories or think them away, but we can learn further from them, modify our responses to present situations on the basis of what we have learned, or inhibit our ruminations when we realize they do not necessarily better a current situation or help us learn from it. Sometimes suppressing memories may be healthier than delving into them, especially given that they may bias our perceptions, interpretation of a current situation, and attention in the present (Daleiden & Vasey, 1997). That is easy for me to say, of course, and I know how bad it feels when loss-related memories suddenly arise. Sometimes we *must* revisit an emotionally distressing memory in order to control it (Depue et al., 2007). We can try to recognize that the way we feel at a given moment may correspond to imagery or thoughts associated with painful memories; we can then find ways to distract ourselves from the feeling and control the urge to revisit the past through our thoughts.[1]

At random times, something completely benign may activate memories that connect us with the departed. For example, when my younger son was born with red hair, I immediately thought of my beloved grandfather's red moustache. Was it a sign that he was there with me? Perhaps it was just an inheritable trait. As this son

---

[1]Prefrontal brain areas associated with inhibitory mechanisms, lateralized predominantly to the right hemisphere, are involved in the suppression of emotional reactivity (Depue et al., 2007). Suppressing retrieval engages the right medial frontal gyrus and reduces related hippocampal activity (M. C. Anderson & Levy, 2009; Depue et al., 2007).

grew older and became interested in mathematics, to the point of achieving a successful career in analytics, I thought of my father's interest in math and how he had always studied in his attempts to learn further. When my older son was in his first year of medical school in New York, he wrote his first paper about rheumatic heart disease because he found the subject interesting. Why did he choose rheumatic heart disease, of all topics? He had no idea that my father's death was due to the illness. When he told me he had chosen to write about it, I recalled memories of my father's choice to reject surgery and die from his illness because he was grief stricken about my mother's death. Yet the fact that my son had chosen this topic also led me to wonder, superstitiously, if my father, whose childhood was associated with New York City, aided my son's admission to the medical school. Thus, was the topic my son chose a message of sorts from my father? Such thinking is completely illogical but, for those of us who are always looking for lost loved ones in strange places, somewhat plausible.

Later in my son's medical school training, as he learned about genetic predispositions to diseases, he suggested that I pursue genetic testing for cancer to inform him and his sibling of their potential vulnerability. While I was waiting for the genetic test results, I encountered unexpected moments of intense sadness and tears one day as I was running in the woods. I feared that my genes contained a time bomb that I had passed on to my children. I also remembered how my mother had suffered. Thankfully, the tests were negative and, in retrospect, it was interesting to me to have such an intense emotional response to memories activated by a genetic test.

Although we can attempt to steer the direction of our thoughts, this may not always be possible. Recurrent and intrusive thoughts disturb people in their early days, weeks, and even months of loss. Intrusive thoughts and pervasive yearning for the deceased are often correlated with a griever's inclination to focus on reminders of the deceased that exacerbate bittersweet memories of shared events and thus on the unattainable goal of reunion.[2]

Intrusive memories involve autobiographical memory and what cognitive psychologists refer to as *involuntary memory* (Brewin et al., 2010). Involuntary memory influences the recall of specific episodes that affect our mood and trigger bodily reactions; therefore, the images associated with intrusive memories tend to be vivid, persistent, hard to control, and accompanied by intense emotional responses (Brewin et al., 2010). Images of scenes related to events that occurred around the death of a loved one, and the meaning of those events, are imprinted in the mind of the survivor (Shuchter & Zisook, 1993). When our attention is not actively engaged, as in the earlier example when Jaelyn went to bed and attempted to drift off to sleep, intrusive images are more likely to emerge. Our cognitive ability to create pictures in our mind can help soothe our feelings around loss, but it can also activate distress. The subject of involuntary memory is discussed in more detail in the next chapter.

It is no wonder that a significant loss may interfere with how we usually process information. Cognitive difficulties in grieving individuals may be related to an interaction between cognition and emotion that temporarily compromises concentration (O'Connor & McConnell, 2018). In the early weeks or months of bereavement, mental disorganization may appear as distractibility, confusion, forgetfulness, and lack of clarity and coherence (Shuchter & Zisook, 1993). People who otherwise consider themselves to be emotionally

---

[2]Differences were found in mourners' regulation of attention and sadness during pangs of grief based on activity in the mourners' amygdalae and prefrontal regulatory regions and connectivity between these brain regions that distinguished relevant differences in grief style (Freed et al., 2009).

strong or resilient may experience a sense of helplessness that is due to the cumulative effects of grief on their mental and emotional lives (Shuchter & Zisook, 1993).

IMAGINATION AND IMAGERY

As each of my children approached the age I had been when my mother died, I recalled childhood scenes in which I had imagined the impossible and then ached for it. Beneath my bedcovers at night, holding an image of my mother in my mind, I had prayed that someday I would have my mommy back again. Decades later, I vividly remembered those childhood scenes upon hearing a jazz vocalist sing "Maybe You'll Be There," a song that describes imagining a hoped-for reunion with a loved one (Bloom & Gallop, 1947).

Throughout my young adulthood, my longing for my father's presence led to auspicious imaginings. By then, with help from inspiring mentors, I had a renewed intellectual verve and the drive to pursue academic goals. Although my father was not alive to witness my accomplishments, I imagined he knew about them and that they might restore the happiness he had lost with my mother's passing. In one instance, I tearfully spoke to him in my mind, hoping that any pride I gave him would lift his spirits. Anything is possible in the imagination, and through imagery we can bring the deceased back to life, so to speak, and attempt to make things different.

"We live on images," wrote Robert Lifton (1979, p. 3), the distinguished psychiatrist and author, who described the elusive psychological relationship between death and the flow of life. *Imagery* is a cognitive process that enables humans to construct visual, sensory, or imaginative scenes that otherwise reside in memory (McBride & Cutting, 2016). Images can possess sensory qualities related to vision, hearing, taste, smell, touch, and movement (Hackmann, 1998; Kosslyn, 1994). Aside from their presence in fantasies during our waking life, they also occur in our dreams. Through imagery, we can connect possibilities that we hope to realize or duplicate (Tomkins, 2008). In this way, we can create images that reunite us with someone who has died.

Mental imagery enables grievers to relieve the effects of distress and remain close to the departed. For instance, in the early months of grieving, whenever Shannon walked by the chair where, most evenings, her husband had sat reading, she could "see" him there. Similarly, at night she would "hear" him breathing next to her. A sense of presence may be felt as a comforting nearness, an awareness of warmth, a sense of sacredness, or sometimes as a frightening perception of a ghost or specter (Datson & Marwit, 1997; Parker, 2005; Parkes, 1970; Rees, 2001; Sormanti & August, 1997; Steffen & Coyle, 2010).

In childhood, fertile imagery may represent a coping mechanism in response to loss. Whereas some children who experience loss may immerse themselves in everyday activities, others may enact their emotional states, which the adults in their lives may perceive as behavioral problems. Some others may retreat to fantasies of seeing the lost parent again. Past theorists have maintained that mourning is not possible in young children and that adolescence is a developmental precondition for mourning (e.g., Wolfenstein, 1966). Our understanding of this is evolving, however; I find we must alter our perceptions of mourning to allow for the responses of children.

Attachment researcher John Bowlby (1961) explained that when children protest in reaction to loss and demand the lost loved one's return, they are displaying a painful awareness of irretrievability, yet also they are stepping toward accepting reality. They will eventually tolerate the idea of giving up the deceased (Bowlby, 1961). Although I agree that an eventual awareness of irretrievability does take place with children, I question whether the lost love object is ever "given up."

Children do mourn, often silently, and somehow they come to believe that grief is something we process and get over. Many years ago, I hosted a weekly call-in talk show for children on Radio Disney stations, known as "KidTalk With Dr. Mary" (Lamia, 2006). Several of the programs focused on the subject of loss. Not surprisingly, many callers were concerned about their continued or intermittent sadness over the death of a person or pet. One 8-year-old boy told me that his grandfather had died 2 weeks before, and he wanted to know "how to get over it." He said he thought about his grandfather "all the time and can't concentrate on anything else." A 12-year-old boy explained that his dog had died, and he wanted to know what to do, since he couldn't say goodbye to her. He added, "I don't think I could ever fill my heart with what is left of her." I didn't ask what he meant by his choice of words; however, I felt their meaning. A 13-year-old girl said that since her mom died several years ago, her dad tries to be both a mom and dad, adding, "but it always feels like something is missing." She asked, "How do I get over my mom dying?" All of these children were grappling with the idea of a process they must go through.

The silently held aspects of grief, especially among children, have perhaps obscured our understanding of what actually takes place: They remember, and mourn, yet are unlikely to tell us about it. They do not get over grief. Much like adults remember the idealized version of a loved one who has died, children also tend to idealize a deceased parent. Idealized or not, in a child's creative mind a deceased parent is the one the child knows and whose image continues to guide the child's life, for better or worse. Early theorists did not consider that children who lose a parent early in life may continue their bond with the parent long after they acknowledge to themselves that the parent will never return. Using imagination and imagery, children keep their loved ones close in waking life as well as in their dreams. They struggle with the process of getting over grief because they never truly get over it; instead, they silently continue their bonds with a loved one.

CONTINUING BONDS

Perhaps in our attempts to make sense of grief we have ignored the processes that happen organically in human memory. For instance, the process of folding new information into memory involves reinterpreting a new experience so that it fits with preexisting information. One way to resolve the dissonance between memories of someone who was once living with the reality of their absence in the present is to create a *continuing bond*.

Thought helps us find ways to continue our bonds with people we love and have forever lost. Some people focus on a sign or signal of a loved one's presence, such as the blooming of an orchid on the anniversary of a death, a hummingbird fluttering at the window, or my son's choice of topics for a paper. Others privately communicate with departed loved ones through fantasies, prayers, rituals, holy objects, or conversations. Clients have described to me the "altars" they have created, such as a table with items of the deceased that honors their memory. One person told me that he plays the favorite music of a lost friend to "spend time with him." Indeed, we can imagine our way into an ongoing relationship with the deceased.

Our inner dialogues with the dead are often part of the silence we keep. It seems that such revelations require an implicit trust that grievers may not have in other people. I have always felt privileged when clients reveal the various ways they have continued a relationship with the deceased, possibly sensing that I would not deem what they say as indicative of pathology. I have heard varied narratives of experiences that somehow represent a loved one, from finding feathers or pennies to elaborate circumstances that have led the person to feel the presence of someone who has died. Although I have been there, too, disclosing my own experiences was never required, and I certainly would not have imposed them on my clients.

I have, however, often conveyed that sensing the presence of someone is reminiscent of the attachment and security we once felt and may need at the present moment.

Just as emotions can influence our thoughts, our thoughts and perceptions can influence our emotions. Particular beliefs related to our culture, religion, and the environment in which we live affect the thoughts we assign to situations; therefore, our cognitive perception of a situation may determine how we interpret and respond emotionally to it (J. S. Beck, 2011). For example, if we believe people who have died are somehow looking after us, we may interpret a disappointment as something that is ultimately in our best interest based on "their" assessment of the situation. People may use their beliefs to bolster their resilience, and whether or not this is helpful in the long run has yet to be determined.

> **There is a healthy aspect to maintaining a bond with the deceased.**

Although death ends the boundary of a life, it does not end a relationship (Hall, 2014). There is a healthy aspect to maintaining a bond with the deceased, and the severing of bonds may not be necessary (Klass et al., 1996). Continued bonds can offer comfort safety, and support, both during the time of transition and afterward. If we can use our memories to restore a lost connection, then imagining the person is still here with us in some way can be a pillar of support and a source of comfort. Many people have an occasionally one-sided conversation with someone who has died, assuming the departed can hear them or can help them. If we consider that we learned something from the relationship when the person was alive, we can continue learning through our memories of them as well as through any inferences we make about how they would respond. I certainly needed the continuing bonds I had with my parents after their deaths. When one is vulnerable, calling up memories of someone as a source of hope or protection can create a sense of stability, a feeling that they are still here with us. We don't know if the deceased are actually with us, of course. In my own mind, it does not matter.

Researchers have examined whether continuing a bond with the departed is adaptive or obstructive. Who benefits from maintaining ties to the deceased, or relinquishing them, continues to be an area of study (Stroebe & Schut, 2005). For example, researchers have found more significant separation distress in survivors who have strong continuing bonds but cannot make personal, practical, existential, or spiritual sense of their losses (Neimeyer et al., 2006). In this way, a continuing bond can trap some people in past experiences. Similarly, I have seen clients who have missed a lost loved one so much that they fall asleep, hoping to have a dream about them that will continue the relationship. The departed, however, are a static image represented in memory, not necessarily as who they were but as we perceived them. Any continued relationship with them involves retrieving memories to represent them in our thoughts or even in our dreams. A sad truth regarding continued bonds is that the deceased no longer grow with us, at least as far as we know.

THINKING OUR WAY INTO MEANINGS

In the past, experts on grief have suggested that people confront the reality of their loss, review events that occurred around that time, focus on memories, and work toward detachment from the deceased (Stroebe & Stroebe, 1991). Thankfully, contemporary bereavement research has shifted the goals for the bereaved, focusing instead on how we make sense of our suffering, find meaning in loss, and reconsider who we are (Neimeyer & Thompson, 2014; Strecher, 2016). The concept of *meaning making* (sometimes called *sense making*), technically referred to as "cognitive semiotics," has a long history dating from Ancient Greece to today's cognitive sciences and psychological studies (Konderak, 2019). The tradition of cognitive semiotics concerns *dynamic meaning making*, which refers to how meanings change, rather than freezing a particular significance at a given moment (Konderak, 2019).

Emotions are meanings. Grief is an emotional meaning in and of itself. How we respond to loss takes the meaning in a particular direction. Theoretical physicist David Bohm (1987) defined the word "meaning" as involving our application of significance and value to something, which then determines an action, intention, or purpose. Throughout life, the significance we bestow on a specific event is what turns the event into an experience with the potential to change us (J. Smith, 2018). Along with the experiential significance of what has happened, we may apply an existential meaning that involves what the event means for our identity or who we are (J. Smith, 2018). Furthermore, we may consider the meaning in terms of our life purpose or the meaning of our life (J. Smith, 2018). In the case of loss, we may ask, "What does it mean to me that my loved one has died?" "What does this mean in terms of who I am?" and "What does my life mean without this person?"

Some contemporary meaning making allows us to explore our core values and find a bigger purpose than ourselves, making sense of loss by seeking an explanation that corresponds to the griever's worldview or by discovering ways to derive positive benefits, or even change, from the loss (C. G. Davis et al., 1998; Gillies & Neimeyer, 2006; Neimeyer & Sands, 2011). According to bereavement researchers, narrative strategies that create meaning regarding loss, such as making links, drawing insight, and overcoming the distress of disharmonious elements in our narratives, can lessen bereavement complications for mourners and even promote adjustment (Bonanno et al., 2005; Helgeson et al., 2006; Neimeyer, 2001). Thus, through the narrative processing of memories whereby we self-reflectively tell our story, we transform autobiographical memories into a sense of self that provides us with feelings of coherence, individuality, and unity (Prebble et al., 2013).

Other bereavement researchers, however, have questioned the centrality of sense making and finding meaning in the wake of loss. In some cases, people believe their losses do not make sense because the death of a loved one seems unjust, random, or unfair (Lewis Hall & Hill, 2019). In other cases, a loss may be consistent with the individual's worldview, so making sense of it is not required for coping (Lewis Hall & Hill, 2019). Furthermore, the griever's attempt to make meaning of loss may be unsuccessful and instead lead to ruminative thinking (Michael & Snyder, 2005). Moreover, meaning making does not necessarily correlate with happiness, even though extracting meaning from our life narratives may lead to positive dimensions of our personality, stress-related growth, and fulfilling life choices (Singer, 2004).

Grief is not something we necessarily get over even when we do create meaning or make sense of it. Meaning making can give grief a purpose through a life of its own. For example, some people take on an endeavor after suffering a loss that serves others' lives and therefore enhances the richness of their own life, such as starting a charity to help others whose loved ones have a particular illness. If I perceive my work as a psychologist as honoring my father by "healing broken hearts," even though this is not the case, I have derived a value and a purpose from my grief; however, any altruistic motives do not erase what I feel.

In some situations, the meaning making or sense making in response to grief may involve cultural, religious, or personal imagery that may be labeled by some clinicians or researchers as pathological. Indeed, we often attempt to account for what happens to us by applying some meaning to what has happened and to the emotions we experience. Perhaps some examples will clarify this viewpoint. Early in my therapy practice, I saw several women whose gynecological problems had resulted in surgery to remove their uterus and ovaries. Today, a total hysterectomy would be an unlikely recommendation for the particular gynecological issues these women had at the time. After surgery, these women sought help for strange occurrences in their lives. Their narratives differed, but the contexts were similar. All of these clients maintained a strong conviction that something had been stolen from them or had mysteriously gone missing. Jewelry had been stolen from a locked jewelry box, money that had been hidden away was gone, an item of value that had always been in a particular place had been taken. Were these matters of disordered thinking that required medication? If we consider their emotional response to this significant (and likely unnecessary) surgery, and the cognitions that created a symbolic meaning or made sense of how these women felt, the loss of the capability to have a child would certainly translate into something of value having been taken or stolen. Women who long to have children but are unable to conceive, along with childless men who want offspring, are among those who silently grieve for what could have been. The powerful desire to become a parent, or the idealization of parenthood, often makes deriving positive meaning from such situations impossible.

Given the myriad ways that loss is internally represented, how we make sense of loss may not seem logical to most other people. Cultural and religious beliefs, along with folklore, fantasy, and various imaginings, influence our values, sense making of loss, and the meaning we attribute to it. In my case, meaning making and sense making regarding my parents' death were complicated by all of these factors. As described in Chapter 1, my mother was fascinated by dream imagery. She often ushered in the morning by inviting my father, brother, and me to share our dreams, interpreting them with the book she had brought with her from Italy. After my grandmother's death, when I was 5, my mother would occasionally tell us another episode of her recurring dream that my grandmother was calling her to heaven. My mother's recurring dream was an anchor for sense making, but it was far beyond my comprehension at the time.

My mother's dream of her mother calling her to heaven, along with her reporting the dream to our family, may unknowingly have served many purposes. From an academic perspective, my mother's dream may have been a way to account for her limited life expectancy; remain attached to her mother, who had recently died; and prepare my father, brother, and me for her impending death. From the standpoint of sense making based on my mother's personal, cultural, and religious beliefs, however, the dream was a message concerning her fate: My grandmother could not be without her and was calling her to heaven. Keep in mind that my mother's initial cancer diagnosis coincided with the death of her mother the following year. My mother and grandmother were extremely close. My grandmother and her young family had taken the long journey by ship from Italy to America, like many who fled Sicily's poverty, where they joined my grandfather. In the early 1920s, migrating from Italy to America meant enduring the cramped quarters of the ship's steerage section, where people sat on their trunks for many days.

At the vigil Mass after my mother's death, my father gave credence to the dream message sent from heaven by my grandmother. Near the conclusion of the Mass, just as the priest began to close the cover of my mother's casket, my father suddenly stood up. Looking toward the ceiling of the dark mortuary and extending his arms upward, with anguish he bellowed to my dead grandmother, "Now you have her, I hope you're satisfied." Then he crumbled and wept.

My father's sense making of my mother's death was certainly influenced by his Sicilian superstitions and Catholicism. Even at age 11, I sort of knew such thinking was illogical. But did I? On the basis of subsequent events, it seems that my mother's dream, coupled with my father's dramatic emotional display at her vigil Mass, planted a seed in my memory where illogical beliefs can take hold. Those seemingly insignificant seeds began to grow in my late adolescence and then blossomed into my own recurring dream:

I am standing on a wood-planked path of a harbor, surrounded by darkness and fog. Looking through the mist, I see a large boat tied to a dock. Two women wearing long coats and with kerchiefs covering their heads are on the deck of the ship. Their clothing resembles what my mother and grandmother had worn in cold winter months. Using arm movements, they are summoning me to board the vessel. I pause, then turn and walk away, resisting the allure to go with them. I feel a sense of guilt and emptiness, along with indistinct hope.

I could defy my mother only in my dreams. Nonetheless, dreams can cast our memories and present concerns into future scenes that guide us. This particular recurring dream gave me hope that, unlike my mother and grandmother, I could live a full life.

In any case, I maintain that dream imagery about someone who has died is a "visit" of sorts, but it is a visit from a place inside of us— our memories—where the person now lives. Dreams are imaginal representations of what resides in our implicit and autobiographical memories that become activated by a present stimulus—for example, an event, a relationship, or a thought. Thus, my recurring dream likely reflected one of the many days when I wondered if I would live beyond my mother's age at death. Some researchers who deal with dreams and meaning making claim that grief dreams are spiritually transformative visits from our loved ones that bring us reassurance and comfort (cf. Ni, 2016).

Vague sensory memories of the people we have lost remain, much like a faint scar on new skin can remind us of an old painful wound.

Despite my rational convictions, when I had this recurring dream I wondered if maybe, just maybe, it was a message from my mother and grandmother. After all, I was well programmed by my parents' belief in the divine prophecy conveyed by my mother's dream. Cognitively, I knew better, and emotionally I did not. Even now, using cognitive processes, I can describe how memories and current circumstances create dream imagery, yet at the same time, internally I still feel tiny remnants of a sensation that is loyal to the meanings my parents constructed. We can use our cognitive and perceptual processes to reinterpret a memory of a situation or an event, which may enable us to feel differently about it emotionally (J. S. Beck, 2011), yet vague sensory memories of the people we lost remain, much like a faint scar on new skin can remind us of an old painful wound.

It is essential to consider how we derive meaning from life after loss.

Perhaps deliberate attempts to find meaning in loss and make sense of it may represent a cognitive bias that neglects how the emotional meanings related to the deceased person influence how we think and feel and how they change inside us. Thus, alongside any attempt to make meaning from our loss, in particular the notion that we create a meaning that honors those we have lost, it is essential to consider *how we derive meaning from life after loss*. After a significant loss we naturally may be prone to amplify the importance of the departed, yet the meaning of our lives is not determined by any one person, and it may even be unfair to burden anyone with that responsibility. Thus, the challenge for all of us is not so much to find meaning in our loss but to discover or rediscover meaning in our lives without them.

REGRET AND UNFINISHED BUSINESS

Bereavement-related regret and unfinished business involve wondering how something might have been if we had acted otherwise. Sometimes we wish we had done a particular thing, or refrained from taking some action; other times, we sense that we left something unsaid (Bonanno et al., 2004; FitzGibbon et al., 2021; Holland et al., 2014, 2020; Klingspon et al., 2015; Torges et al., 2008). Naturally, anyone who anticipates more years with a loved one is left with the unfinished business of life itself if the loved one is suddenly gone. Similarly, regret conveys that some different circumstance may have eased our postloss distress. Regret contains a strong motivational lure in that we cannot keep ourselves from considering alternatives and seeking information about them (FitzGibbon et al., 2021).

When my children were young, I recalled a scene from my childhood in which my mother was sitting on the couch, her head back, and appearing half-asleep. Around that time, she often seemed distracted or uninvolved. The meaning I attributed to this unusual disconnection from her was that perhaps she loved me less than she loved my brother, or that maybe I was a disappointment so she did not love me anymore. In this particular instance, I sat across the room and made up a few lines of a song about not being loved. Because she didn't stir, I assumed she was sleeping and that maybe a dream would tell her about my hurt feelings given that I was unable to tell her myself.

Sadly, and regretfully, I realized many years later that these memories of a broken bond with my mother came when she was suffering from the effects of metastasized cancer. Although my new perspective altered how I felt, I regretted that I had not known she was very ill and did not take care of her somehow. Thus, regret is associated with memories of our personal history linked with our imagining better outcomes if we had lived the past differently.

Regret has been conceptualized as a "higher order cognitive emotion" because it involves both thinking and feeling (Lerner & Keltner, 2001; Västfjäll et al., 2011). Dominant emotions in regret are shame and distress/sadness. Because these emotions are repeatedly activated, they can produce a mood. When we experience the shame of regret, we are motivated to temporarily alter memories by imagining what might have been had we taken a different path or seized an opportunity (Nathanson, 1992). Although we cannot erase the past, considering the choices we made and the alternative possibilities can help us learn something for the future and so can shape us in a positive way.

We may, however, ignore the lessons we can learn from regret. We may instead cope with, or defend against, the shame we feel over an error or misunderstanding by attacking the other, attacking ourselves, and through withdrawal or avoidance (Nathanson, 1992). When someone disappears from our life, we may encounter unanticipated regrets or unfinished business. Surviving spouses may regret that the spouse who died could not have continued to live a healthy and happy life, or they may dwell on past decisions and missed opportunities (Shuchter & Zisook, 1993). If we resort to defensive responses to the shame involved in regret and unfinished business, we may attack ourselves (e.g., "I should have taken him to another specialist" or "I should have told her that I appreciated our friendship"). We may attack the deceased (e.g., "I'm so mad at him for not taking care of his health"). We may use avoidance (e.g., "I'm just going to have a few drinks to feel better"), or we may withdraw (e.g., "I can't stand the idea of going anywhere without my partner" or "I'll never take that trip").

Our regrets inform us of a failure to live up to our ideals, over and above the mistakes we have made (Davidai & Gilovich, 2018). In the long run, we regret our inactions more than our actions, so regret lingers where opportunity existed and where we have missed tangible prospects for change, growth, and renewal (Davidai & Gilovich, 2018; Roese & Summerville, 2005). Despite how uncomfortable regrets and unfinished business may feel, they represent internal feedback about our past behavior. The cognitive process, known as *counterfactual thinking*, has to do with our assessment of an outcome as compared with what would have been gained or lost had we made a different decision (Zeelenberg et al., 1998). We mentally simulate other outcomes to past events by considering hypothetical alternatives (C. G. Davis et al., 1995). For example, we often hear that a loved one might still be alive if an alternative decision had been made or if some action had taken place, such as seeing a different doctor or responding sooner to a symptom. Thus, regret may represent an important aspect of our capacity to review our decisions or to assess our behaviors retrospectively. Alternatively, it may exemplify our inclination to pursue counterfactual information for its own sake (FitzGibbon et al., 2021). After we experience a loss we often consider what we could have done differently, knowing we cannot undo the past yet recognizing we can learn from it.

The shame of regret may feel terrible, but it is a teacher that enables us to look inside and to think deeply about ourselves (Nathanson, 1992). Regret provides an opportunity for self-reflection and is a way to derive meaning from our experiences. Although looking back may not always influence future behavior, especially when it involves the departed, it can be a learning experience. This self-reflective capacity can enable us to positively respond to hardship.

Next, let's look at our sensory memories and how they may interface with physiological bereavement-related responses. How does grief remain present within our sensory memories and in our body? Many people with health-related concerns are not aware that they are attempting to cope with their feelings. Chapter 6 addresses the sensory memories and physiological effects related to grief.

TO SUMMARIZE

Grief is mysterious because it represents the unique life stories from which it emerges. How we think and what we believe are important to our understanding of grief. Early grief periods may involve cognitive disruptions, such as cloudy thinking, intrusive images, repetitive thoughts, or attention and concentration difficulties. Severe stress can negatively affect memory, and reminiscing about exciting or joyful past experiences shared with the departed may be experienced as bittersweet. Sometimes, suppressing painful memories can reduce our emotional responses to disturbing images and scenes.

Continuing relationships with the departed may occur through fantasies, prayers, rituals, conversations, or through beliefs that a person lost is with us. Mental imagery enables grievers to relieve the effects of distress and longing and to remain close to the departed by creating perceptual representations of experiences in their minds. Researchers and theorists have not always agreed about whether continuing a bond with the departed is adaptive or obstructive.

We tend to seek meaning in what happens to us and make sense of our experiences. The narratives we construct are based on autobiographical memories. Dream imagery about someone who has died is a visit from a place inside of us: our memories. Regret is another aspect of our cognitive response to loss. Despite how negative regret may feel, it represents internal feedback about our past behavior.

Reflections

- If you maintain a continued bond with someone who has died, what are the ways in which this relationship with them has helped you?
- What does it mean to you that your loved one has died? What does this mean in terms of who you are? What gave your life meaning prior to the loss of a loved one? What meaning do you seek or find in your life now that the person you loved has died?
- Do you recall a dream that you interpreted as a "visit" from a loved one that has symbolic meaning for you? If you look back at the dream, what was the central theme? What was going on in your life the day of the dream, or the day before, that may relate to it?
- What regrets do you have regarding the loss of a loved one? Do you find that you attack yourself, attack others, withdraw, or use avoidance rather than attempt to learn from what you regret? If learning from regret is a goal, what is it that you have learned from the experience?

CHAPTER 6

SENSORY AND PHYSIOLOGICAL REMINDERS

I find the scent of cut flowers in a small space suffocating. The redolence evokes sensations I felt in the dimly lit mortuary where my mother lay surrounded by roses, carnations, and lilies. British author Beverley Nichols (1951) wrote, "To be overcome by the fragrance of flowers is a delectable form of defeat" (p. 240). For me, the consuming scent of flowers involved surrendering to hopelessness. Yet a whiff of the aroma emanating from a pipe or cigar enchants me, inducing warm sensations reminiscent of my father and grandfather, whose images are obscured within exhaled billows of smoke.

Our senses of smell, taste, touch, sight, and hearing can take us on a journey into memory. Among our many senses, smell and taste are the most common priming sources, serving as a medium between a stimulus and a representation that exists in memory. Humans are constantly relating the past to the present by turning their sensory perceptions inward to memory and thought or by turning memory outward to their senses (Tomkins, 2008). Thus, our memory retrieval skills enable us to match the past with the present, just as our perceptual skills enable us to connect a stimulus in the present to an event in the past.

Many of the sensory memories we recall show how unexpectedly our daily experiences can trigger loss-related reminders. For example, Harrison, who had lost his adult son, saw a bird taking a bath in rainwater on the side of a street. He instantly and sadly recalled a scene with his son, who as a gentle little boy loved watching the birds in their yard. Harrison wondered whether seeing the bird would have led him to recall the memory if his son were still living. Perhaps the loss of a loved one primes our awareness of sensory cues that access memories of the deceased, as though in the back of our minds we are always looking for those whom we have lost.

Intimate relationships can become regulators of our internal biological processes. Loss can result in biologic changes in the survivor, even resulting physical conditions or symptoms that suggest medical illness. Physiological effects of loss include immune imbalance, altered sleep, inflammatory cell mobilization, and changes in heart rate or blood pressure. In this chapter, we specifically explore the sensory memories and physiological responses that result from loss.

SENSORY MEMORY

Sensory memory refers to the impressions we form and maintain of stimuli we perceive through our senses. Many of us have learned that humans have five senses with corresponding memory, including smell (olfactory memory), touch (haptic memory), taste (gustatory memory), vision (iconic memory), or hearing (auditory/echoic memory). However, if we rightly include the many separable sensory systems of touch (light touch, pressure, cold, heat, pain, itch), the vestibular system (balance, posture, and orientation), and proprioception (muscles and awareness of one's position and movement), the human body actually has anywhere from seven to 12 sensory systems (Schwartz & Krantz, 2016).

When sensory input becomes processed in the brain and is turned into a conscious experience that provides usable information, we refer to it as *perception* (Schwartz & Krantz, 2016). Sensation and perception are highly complex processes that are far beyond the scope of this book; however, what is important in relation to grief is that all of our perceptions involve *phenomenology*—the subjective and private experience of what we perceive in the world around us (Schwartz & Krantz, 2016). Although we may share similar referents or names for what we perceive, be it a cigar or "anguish," we do not have the same phenomenological experience regarding the person, place, or thing. Thus, my phenomenological experience in smelling cigar smoke would be different from everyone else's given that it is based on my personal history, culture, and the environment in which I was raised. Likewise, our sensory, perceptual, and emotional experiences of anguish are phenomenologically unique. Nonetheless, we do share some similarities that involve how we function as humans.

When loss is a distant memory, present sensory experiences may reawaken images that affect our current emotional, cognitive, and physiological responses. The process of reactivating an image from explicit memory, based on its similarity to a current sensory cue or our present state of mind, is called *ecphory*, or an *ecphoric sensation* (Tulving, 1993). As an example, one day while walking in San Diego, I happened to see two elderly men who were sitting on a bench smoking cigars and speaking a foreign language. Whereas many people might attempt to avoid the odor of a cigar, my own bittersweet nostalgic pleasure led me to take a deep breath so that I could get a stronger whiff of the scent, which reminded me of my father and grandfather. Because explicit memories are considered to be context dependent, memory retrieval is enhanced when conditions are similar to those when the memory was initially encoded (Siegel, 2001). In this regard, the context of two elderly men speaking a foreign language also added fuel to my automatic memory retrieval.

Someone could have a background similar to my own—let's say she misses her deceased father, who happened to smoke cigars when she was a child—but she may respond differently on the basis of the rest of her history, the relationship she had with her father, the length of time that has passed since her father's death, or many other factors. This imaginary person could pass the two men smoking cigars, and the memory could activate distress and tears rather than anything similar to my experience of nostalgic pleasure laced with sadness. She may become angry in response to remembering her loss and assume she was cheated out of having a father who lived a long life, which might put her in a bad mood for part of the day. Similarly, whereas one person may assume that encountering the men with cigars is a sign from her father, another person may not attach any meaning to the encounter.

> **The ways we respond to our sensory experiences that evoke loss-related memories are indeed very personal.**

The point is, all of us have an elaborate sensory system that responds to stimuli in our environment. The way we respond emotionally is not right or wrong, better or worse. Our responses depend on how our emotions have been scripted on the basis of prior experiences. The ways we respond to our sensory experiences that evoke loss-related memories are indeed very personal. Let's take a look at some of the other ways our sensory memories may become activated and how we may respond to them.

OLFACTORY (SMELL-RELATED) MEMORY

We regard our nose primarily as the bodily apparatus that enables us to smell; however, olfactory information is actually processed in the emotional and memory centers of the brain. Thus, our nose is an implement that admits smells to olfactory nerves, initiating a complex process within the brain whereby odors constitute an emotional experience.

A particular odor can quickly trigger autobiographical memories, such as emotions and images from childhood or the memory of a loved one who has died.

The processing of olfactory information begins in the *cribriform plate*—a small structure near the top of the head that lies along the base of the skull. If you have ever wondered why people who sustain an injury near their forehead temporarily lose their sense of smell, it is because they have likely fractured their cribriform plate.[1] Nerve cells transmit information from the cribriform plate to parts of the brain involving memory and emotion[2]; consequently, a particular odor can quickly trigger autobiographical memories, such as emotions and images from childhood or the memory of a loved one who has died.

Loss-related memories of our experiences with smells can become activated by present circumstances that match stored information, such as my response to the smell of flowers or cigar smoke. As a result,

---

[1]Schwartz and Krantz (2016) explained how injuries can sever the axons (nerve cells that transmit information) that are projected from olfactory receptor neurons through the sieve-like holes in the cribriform plate and converge to form the olfactory nerve.

[2]Herz et al. (2004) illustrated how axons project further, connecting to parts of the brain involving memory and emotion, specifically, the amygdala and the piriform cortex. The emotional effects of odors are also influenced by the projection of nerve cells into the right orbitofrontal cortex. Among its functions, the right orbitofrontal cortex informs us to approach or distance ourselves from an odor because of how it makes us feel, and integrates the smell and taste of food.

various odors can increase our heart rate or elevate our blood pressure. On the other hand, something we smell can lower our heart rate and blood pressure, thereby creating a sense of well-being or calmness.

Sleep Disruption and Olfactory Memory

If certain smells can affect us physiologically and emotionally in our waking life, can they also influence our sleep? Disrupted sleep and stress are often cited among people whose romantic partner dies. In an international study across diverse cultures, sleep disturbances were among the most frequently reported bereavement symptoms (Simon et al., 1999). We may attribute these symptoms to many causes, but we may not consider how the absence of a loved one's smell plays a role. According to recent research, though, the scent of a loved one may influence our response to stress and how well we sleep (M. K. Hofer et al., 2020; McBurney et al., 2006).

In a study that exposed participants to stress, one group sniffed a shirt worn by their romantic partners, and another group sniffed a shirt worn by a stranger. Those who smelled a partner's body odor reported experiencing less stress (M. K. Hofer et al., 2018). In another sleep-related study, people who were involved in romantic relationships slept alone with a t-shirt on their pillow that had either been previously worn by a romantic partner or not (M. K. Hofer & Chen, 2020). The sleep efficiency results for female sleepers, but not male sleepers, were much higher on the nights the t-shirt had the scent of their partners. The researchers speculated that the sleep-inducing and stress-buffering effects of a partner's scent involved perceiving a romantic partner as a source of comfort.

Altering Olfactory Memories of Loss

Evolutionarily speaking, olfactory memories protect us by alerting us to threats or opportunities that can then guide our choices. The childhood memories I described at the beginning of this chapter represent my brain doing what it was programmed to do, even though it is kind of difficult to imagine cigar smoke being associated with pleasure and the scent of flowers signaling distress.

New experiences can alter our response to old sensory memories. The fact is, my mother loved flowers, and her garden was filled with them. I loved the smell of flowers until they became associated with her death. So my response to the fragrance of flowers shifted from pleasurable to distressing, and, fortunately, back again to pleasurable based on a subsequent experience. Later in my life, I became captivated by trickling fountains and blossoms in a peaceful little flower shop near my home. Over time, the fragrance of flowers became linked to the enjoyment I experienced in the shop and my fondness for its owner, although early in my life I developed a strong allergic reaction to the scent of lilies that has never resolved.

> **The passing of time, in which we form new associations through encountering new events, circumstances, and sensations, is a precondition for adapting to loss.**

Because grief does not mean letting go of a loved one but instead involves our response to emotional memories, those who have recently suffered a significant loss may wonder whether they can or will ever feel differently. If we consider only olfactory memories, the passing of time, during which we form new associations through encountering new events, circumstances, and sensations, is a precondition for adapting to loss. The change in my response to the scent of flowers took more than 30 years, even though I remain allergic to lilies. Along the way, I am certain many other perceptions changed. Thus, we must give ourselves time to have novel experiences that both give us a perspective on old memories and create new memories that seem to dampen our responses to a painful past. We may also feel less at the mercy of memories that activate painful emotions if we can become curious about what is happening within us at a given moment, and better understand our responses.

GUSTATORY (TASTE) MEMORY

More than 40 years ago, during my first pregnancy, I craved something I had not eaten since childhood: a corn dog on a stick. I can imagine some readers wondering if I hurt the developing brain of my unborn child, but I will tell the story. As a young child living in the San Francisco Bay area, I first experienced the taste of a corn dog on a day trip with my parents and brother to visit the Fun House, a prominent attraction at Playland-at-the-Beach.[3] The Fun House was known for a creepy life-sized mechanical woman, "Laughing Sal," at the entrance, and a steep wooden slide inside the building. Riding down the slide on a burlap sack with my father was a thrilling moment in my young life and in my attachment to him.

During the pregnancy, I lived less than a mile away from the little hut at Ocean Beach that still sold corn dogs, despite the demolition of the Fun House and the amusement park. At times, I was compelled to buy a corn dog, finding myself consuming it with the pleasure of a child. I recalled my mother later making them, likely in an effort to avoid going to the amusement park ever again.

I eventually realized that my interest in corn dogs actually had to do with longing to have my parents alive to witness the birth of their first grandchild. Amusing stories about cravings in pregnant women are common, although after that time I often wondered whether

---

[3]For an interesting digital archive of San Francisco's former Playland-at-the-Beach, see https://www.foundsf.org/index.php?title=Playland

such "hungers" have something to do with early childhood memories and various longings. We are all different. In my case, the corn dogs brought forth involuntary memories of an idyllic time with my parents during a special time I wished I could share with them.

Involuntary Memory, Taste Sensations, and Loss

The concept of involuntary memory introduced in Chapter 5 is attributed not to neuroscientists but to the French novelist, essayist, and literary critic Marcel Proust. Proust experienced death as a constant presence in human life, yet he also recognized that involuntary memory enables emotional continuity and is a remedy against death and the passing of time, allowing us to taste a piece of eternity (Marčetić, 2017). In the early 1900s, Marcel Proust published a 4,300-page novel, *In Search of Lost Time*, in which he wrote about the involuntary memories activated from tasting a madeleine:

> One day in winter, on my return home, my mother, seeing that I was cold, offered me some tea, a thing I did not ordinarily take. I declined at first, and then, for no particular reason, changed my mind. She sent for one of those squat, plump little cakes called "petites madeleines," which look as though they had been moulded in the fluted valve of a scallop shell. And soon, mechanically, dispirited after a dreary day with the prospect of a depressing morrow, I raised to my lips a spoonful of the tea in which I had soaked a morsel of the cake. No sooner had the warm liquid mixed with the crumbs touched my palate than a shudder ran through me and I stopped, intent upon the extraordinary thing that was happening to me. An exquisite pleasure had invaded my senses, something isolated, detached, with no suggestion of its origin. And at once the vicissitudes of life had become indifferent to me, its disasters innocuous, its brevity illusory—this new sensation having had on me the effect which love has of filling me with a precious essence; or rather this

essence was not in me it was me. I had ceased now to feel mediocre, contingent, mortal. Whence could it have come to me, this
all-powerful joy? I sensed that it was connected with the taste
of the tea and the cake, but that it infinitely transcended those
savors . . . I drink a second mouthful, in which I find nothing
more than in the first, then a third, which gives me rather less
than the second. It is time to stop; the potion is losing it magic.
It is plain that the truth I am seeking lies not in the cup but in
myself. (Proust, 1928, pp. 48–51)

Involuntary memories, also known as *involuntary explicit
memory, involuntary autobiographical memory, involuntary conscious memory*, and "the Proust phenomenon," occur without our
conscious effort when certain cues encountered in everyday life, such
as taste, trigger recollections of the past (see Marčetić, 2017).[4] Taste
involves recognition and memory, and numerous sensorial experiences can become activated once food reaches the mouth and is
experienced as bitter, sweet, salty, sour, or umami (i.e., the flavor of
glutamates; Miranda, 2012; Scott, 2005).

Proust (1928) pointed out at the end of this narrative how a
repetitive sensory experience—in this case, taste—alters our perceptual and phenomenological responses. Humans develop perceptual
skills on the basis of a mechanism in our brain that can select redundancies and other trends across time from the flow of sensory messages (Tomkins, 2008). As a result, eventually we do not attend to
the details of certain habitual sensory input. For example, if we eat
the same dinner every night for a month, our attention to certain
flavors and textures may be heightened at the first meal, but they
will become progressively less noticeable by the end of the month.

---

[4]Miranda (2012) explained that two important brain structures associated
with emotion, the insular cortex and the amygdala, are involved in appeti-
tive and aversive taste memory formation.

> **The valley of our perceptual and phenomenological responses to someone is a human tendency, rather than a personal fault.**

Unfortunately, such perceptual skill, although part of our evolutionary makeup, may cost us when it is linked to appreciation of another person with whom we have lived. Just as we do not "taste" a certain meal we have been eating for a month, we may also become habituated to a close relationship with someone, such as a spouse, partner, or parent. Thus, if they die, we may believe we have undervalued the person most important to us, when it is merely that our brain had become familiar with them. Regrets follow in the form of wishing we had been more attentive, or spent more time with them, or had more overtly expressed and appreciated their value. Nevertheless, this valley of our perceptual and phenomenological responses to someone is a human tendency, not a personal fault.

Appetite and Loss

Appetite disturbances in both children and adults are a commonly recognized symptom of grief. Because the sensory mechanisms induced by eating also include the context of consuming food, such as where and how food is eaten, and with whom, we might expect that the loss of a loved one could influence the survivor's appetite and response to food in general. For example, if we always eat dinner with a spouse, partner, or child, their absence may be painfully conspicuous during mealtimes, aside from the general distress that can affect our appetite. Structure is important in our lives, yet we do not often consider that our memories of a lost loved one become activated during everyday activities such as cooking or eating.

Events that involve a favorite food of a deceased loved one have the potential to trigger a grief response. The same food may eventually be eaten with pleasurable reminders, but that takes time. For example, Sheryl and her husband always looked forward to eating eggs Benedict at his cousin's home on New Year's Day. The mere idea of eating eggs Benedict filled her with sorrow. In the first year after his loss, she avoided the New Year's gathering, knowing how devastated she would feel without her husband present. She could not imagine looking at the eggs without sobbing. Instead of staying home alone, which seemed equally painful, she made arrangements to celebrate the new year by taking a long walk with a friend.

Some people might say that Sheryl should be strong, face the event, eat the eggs Benedict, and deal with her sadness. Such exposure, long before we have adapted to loss is not only painful but adds another painful memory to her already existing ones. Taking the time to accumulate new memories of holidays, if possible, could help her when she returns to the gathering she shared with her husband.

ECHOIC (AUDITORY) MEMORY

When we hear a vocal tone, melody, or a spoken sentence, we find meaning in it through dividing it into words or ideas (Nebenzahl & Albeck, 1990). After hearing the words or sounds several times, their order is memorized, and they enter our long-term memory (Nebenzahl & Albeck, 1990). At will, we can retrieve the stored information. As with other memories, recall of auditory memory often results from an environmental trigger.

The sound of a voice, a song, or a particular noise is a cue that can activate memories. These memories form images in our mind, such as those of a departed person or a circumstance in which they were present. We often do not realize that implicit sensory memories activated by the sound of someone's voice, as well as their smell, may motivate an attachment to them, romantic or otherwise.

Auditory memories are enduring. As an example, listening to music from a certain era brings back memories of our experiences at the time. Upon losing a loved one, hearing a particular piece of shared music can activate joyful memories that lead to a reexperiencing of feelings around the loss. A client whose husband had died 7 years ago told me that, even now, she cannot listen to certain songs they enjoyed together. A reader of my blog posts who had been widowed for several months described an auditory memory:

> Sometimes I feel he is trying to send me a message. . . . Yesterday I heard a beautiful melody in my head. It was so odd, I had to get on the internet to find out what the song was. It turned out to be "Smile" by Nat King Cole. I had not heard that song for decades and certainly did not remember the words.

The lyrics of this song ask us to smile, even when our heart is broken, because there is a promise that tomorrow could be better, and life is still worth living. It is not unusual for the bereaved to have experiences like this reader's. Within our memories are bits of songs that held meaning for us, and without our conscious knowledge these can be triggered by anything in our perceptual and sensory environment. Could the song have been a message from her beloved? In a sense it was, because it signified how he lives in her memories.

The sound of words or music runs deep in our memories. The resonance we experience from certain voices, as well as the irritation we might feel from certain vocal tones, result from implicit and explicit memories of early experiences. For example, my own history led me to focus on vocal tones and rhythms beyond the words that were spoken. Using the excuse that we were American, my parents had refused to teach my brother and me their native Sicilian dialect.

Conveniently, they could converse about my mother's illness and about anything else they wanted to keep secret from us, in Italian. However, *prosodic communications*—vocal tones and rhythms—convey emotion that can be felt by both the intended recipient and a bystander, and these can be more incisive than words. Granted, any felt emotion provides us with only vague information but, even so, I could understand from the vocal tones and rhythm of my parents' conversations that something was wrong, painful, frightening, or eagerly anticipated. Although the experience of being shut out of a conversation may have been difficult for me at the time, I later benefited from it as a psychologist; it enabled me to be hyperattuned to the prosodic communications of my clients.

ICONIC (SIGHT) MEMORY

Whereas one person may be attuned to sounds, another may be vigilant about what is seen. Some researchers have found that our memory for pictures of visual objects is stronger than recognition memory for sounds (Gloede et al., 2017). Interestingly, auditory memory is generally more long lasting, and visual memory seems to have a larger capacity; however, different amounts of experience in our lives with images and sounds may influence the way our memory performs (Gloede et al., 2017). For example, a person who grows up in a family of visual artists or critics may have an active iconic memory if they have learned from the experiences their parents communicated verbally and nonverbally.

> **One of the difficult challenges for people in mourning involves visual cues that trigger memories.**

One of the difficult challenges for people in mourning involves visual cues that trigger memories. A photograph, the belongings of a deceased loved one, or a place where some emotional intimacy was shared can activate memories of pleasurable experiences that result in a grief response. Photographs are like an external memory of moments we have shared with others. As with other sensory input, shortly after a loss a photograph may trigger positive memories that are concurrently very painful. We must decide for ourselves what we can tolerate at any given moment in terms of activating psychological distress or anguish. Instead of believing we should be able to take in a sensory experience, such as looking at an old photograph, without anguish, we should instead make a mental note of our response as a baseline for the next time we do the same. Our level of tolerance for exposing ourselves to visual stimuli that trigger memories of the deceased changes over time and with new life experiences.

For some people, visual reminders are comforting. For example, I have met people who for many years have kept the knickknacks, silver, and antiques of a deceased spouse because they are comforted by them. On the other hand, I know others who are inclined to immediately change their living environment because it activates memories that lead to grief or because they eagerly want to detach from reminders. We are all different, and the choices we make after loss are difficult and intensely personal.

HAPTIC (TOUCH) MEMORY

Unlike other senses, touch requires bodily contact. Sensations of touch arise from the skin, muscles, and other interior senses, yet the skin is considered the primary sense organ whereby touch perception is experienced (Schwartz & Krantz, 2016). *Haptic perception* refers to the process of identifying an object through touch. We do not often consider the vast difference among people when they are

133

identified through touch; however, at some point we may notice distinct differences, for example, in the hugs we receive from others. Whereas some people hug tightly, others hug lightly, some will pat our back as they hug, and so forth. Among the many things that produce longing in the bereaved, hugs from the person who has died seem to be one of the most frequently mentioned in my psychotherapy practice. The absence of touch is also prominent in pet loss.

The physical history shared with a loved one that involves touching, smiling, holding, mutual gaze, erotic or sexual encounters, and emotional attunement become a felt presence that leaves traces in one's own body and lived space (Fuchs, 2018). When these threads of mutual attachment dissolve through loss, the survivor's pain may bear a resemblance to the phantom pain experienced by someone with an amputated limb (Fuchs, 2018).

Can the longing to be touched be relieved by touching? A woman who lost her child wrote the following in response to my blog post: "I rock babies. It's a simple thing. I spend two mornings a week at a day care center that takes infants as young as three months old. There's something so soothing about holding babies."

In general, our bodies respond to the bodies of others who are close to us, which some attachment theorists have described as *coregulation*, namely, a process by which the actions of the other modify our own actions (Butler & Randall, 2013; Fogel & Garvey, 2007). For example, the physical presence of one partner can lead to stress reduction in the other (Butner et al., 2007). Our bodies respond to touch in many different ways. When a loved one dies, we may have a response to the loss of their touch.

THE BODY IN BEREAVEMENT

Many of us have heard about a person who has died shortly after the loss of a long-term partner. In older people, this is commonly known as the *widowhood effect* (Avis et al., 1991). Less well-known are the underlying mechanisms that explain the physical symptoms people experience after a loved one's death. The physical symptoms experienced by some mourners include immune system imbalances, altered sleep, inflammatory cell mobilization, and changes in heart rate or blood pressure (see Buckley et al., 2012; Stroebe et al., 2007; Vitlic et al., 2014). An extreme example was written by a woman in response to one of my blog posts:

> Three months ago I lost my husband of 29 years. I always knew if something happened to him, I would not do well; however, I did not expect this reaction in my wildest dreams. I became physically ill the day he went to hospital. I have been to a neurologist, a hematologist, and now a new internist. All tests are negative, but I feel like I am going to die. I even updated my will and started giving things away. Everyone says "You will get over it" or "Time will heal." That does not apply to me. I truly feel my better half is gone.

The bodily response to the sudden death of a loved one, which may include startle or surprise (often described as *shock*), physical weakness, numbness, or a sense of unreality, may resemble that of a trauma or physical accident (Fuchs, 2018). Typical patterns of bodily symptoms that following the initial response are similar to the heaviness of depression, including bowed gait, shortness of breath, gastrointestinal problems, tightness in the throat, and neurological issues (Fuchs, 2018; Kowalski & Bondmass, 2008; Parkes, 1970). As well, a constant pressure on the chest, experienced as constriction around the heart, may occur in waves of distress (Parkes, 1970).

Human physiological responses to stress involve a part of the brain stem known as the *locus coeruleus*. This site in the brain synthesizes norepinephrine (noradrenaline)—both a stress hormone and a chemical in the body that sends signals between nerve cells. It is a homeostatic control center that influences our attention, cognitive flexibility, decision making, and emotions (Aston-Jones & Cohen, 2005; Beversdorf et al., 1999; Bouret & Sara, 2005). As mentioned in Chapter 5, in the early months of loss, bereaved individuals tend to experience a lack of focus, difficulty making decisions, distraction, and a sense of being unable to find something that is right before their eyes. These symptoms are common responses to the stress of loss.

The stress hormone, cortisol, may be elevated in bereaved individuals, especially in older people, where it has greater potential in regard to immune system alteration, inflammatory markers, and higher heart rate (Buckley et al., 2012; Richardson et al., 2015; Schultze-Florey et al., 2012). Again, the inability to maintain uninterrupted sleep is a problem among grieving individuals; this has been found in studies across several cultures (Buckley et al., 2012). As we would expect, depression worsens the quality of sleep in grieving individuals (Germain et al., 2005). For many bereaved people, maintaining a daily routine that includes healthy eating, exercise, and sleep seems difficult when a loved one has died. Maintaining these everyday behaviors is crucial because they can contribute to one's overall health.

Take a Breath

If there were only a limited number of actions one could take to relieve the bodily response of grief, high on the list would be breathing, alongside exercise and social support. Depressed, anxious, traumatized, and grief-stricken people often do not recognize their unusual or limited breathing patterns any more than the rest of us are conscious of breathing normally. Our experience of the world become linked with bodily responses, and our level of excitation or calm affects our breathing (G. Smith, 2020). When we are anxious, we hold our breath high into the top of the chest, with gradual exhalation that is followed by another breath inhaled high into the chest; the breathing of a depressed person gives the appearance of having longer exhalations than inhalations, which tend to lower the body's energy (G. Smith, 2020). There is a mutually reinforcing effect of breath and mood.

If there were only a limited number of actions one could take to relieve the bodily response of grief, high on the list would be breathing, alongside exercise and social support.

Many books have been written by professionals with expertise in purposeful breathing. In addition, many yoga practices focus on helping people become more conscious of their breathing patterns. Being mindful of our breathing at any given moment may remind us to take a breath, which is good for our lungs, heart, and emotional well-being. When we wither from grief, a deep breath can remind us that we are living. Filling our lungs with air can perhaps make us witness the life that remains within us.

Readers may have, or can easily find, resources that can help them "take a breath." The basic idea is to become aware of your breathing, consciously and intentionally taking in air and exhaling calming breaths every day. Heightening our awareness enables us to notice such things as the parts of our body that move when we breathe, for example, the sensations of air flowing through our nostrils or mouth or the way our posture may affect the depth of our breath (G. Smith, 2020, pp. 19–20). Becoming more aware of our breaths allows us to tune into emotions and alter them. This is especially important when we experience grief.

Partnerships as Internal Regulators

People who live together for a long time develop a biological synchronicity (McClintock, 1971; Sbarra & Hazan, 2008). The loss of a partner can affect what researchers call the "homeostatic regulatory system" of the surviving partner. Human bereavement may result from the withdrawal of specific sensorimotor regulators, such as emotional communication through body posture, facial expression, speech, or hand gestures (M. A. Hofer, 1984). Thus, instead of just investigating the stress imposed by the disruption of an emotional tie between two individuals, we might look carefully at the relationship that existed between the grieving survivor and the person who has died and attempt to understand more precisely who and what has been lost (M. A. Hofer, 1984).

In the aftermath of loss it is important to control states of *physiological dysregulation*—physical changes or disruption in the body and a lowering of resilience—that influence our physical and emotional security. Reaching out for social support, moving toward the establishment of new relationships, and increasing connectedness with family members can help our bodies stay on an even keel (Sbarra & Hazan, 2008). According to one researcher, engaging in physical exercise, yoga, or massage can help prevent the physiological dysregulation and immune problems that occur from a lack of touch (T. Field, 2009). This is not hard to understand. A long walk in nature helps us breathe, tires our muscles, and thus enhances sleep. Granted, it might be hard to put on the hiking boots when we are sad or even agitated. In addition, the search for meaning—how individuals think about, come to understand, and appraise their loss—is considered to be a predictor of physiological arousal control after loss experiences (Sbarra & Hazan, 2008).

Whether we manage a state of dysregulation through physical or social means, some such actions prove to be a chief task in coping with loss. This involves adopting coping strategies that provide a sense of felt security formerly provided by an attachment figure. In some cases, however, it seems impossible to physiologically and emotionally regulate oneself after a loss. My own father is a good example of how loyalty to a partner can obstruct the reorganization of one's life and maintaining one's health. His broken bond with my mother led him to die, in his own personal way, of a broken heart.

Broken Bonds and Broken Hearts

As mentioned in Chapter 2, broken heart syndrome, technically known as *acute stress-induced cardiomyopathy*, involves a physical pain in one's chest or heart that occurs in the presence of acute emotional stress after a significant loss (Mayo Clinic Staff, 2020). The pain is due to a transient dysfunction of the left ventricle, and in most cases the condition is reversible with treatment, although a small percentage of cases may be fatal (Marshall, 2016). When two humans are involved in a deep relationship, they develop what is called a "psychobiological attunement," whereby each person provides both an activating and a calming influence on the other (T. Field, 2012). Stimulation from the partner, including touch and physical intimacy, can enhance this attunement. According to this viewpoint, the loss of a partner may result in physiological disorganization and changes in immune function for the survivor (T. Field et al., 2007). Broken heart syndrome is somewhat difficult to study, given that we do not often have comprehensive data regarding the nature of an individual's relationship with a partner and the person's physical health before the loss.

A primary reason that researchers have used rats and other innocent creatures to study various phenomena is because they cannot ethically do to humans what they propose for their studies. Let's assume a group of researchers want to scientifically study the physiological and biological effects of losing a beloved partner or spouse. First, they would have to systematically assess a number of humans in terms of the strength of their attachment, along with their social, physiological, and neurochemical activity. Next, they would have to do away with the partners or spouses of the participants and then measure the social, physiological, and neurochemical changes that take place in the participants. As you can see, that is impossible.

In this case, enter the little prairie vole as a research participant. Male prairie voles just happen to form enduring social bonds with their female partners, so they may have been ideal subjects for a study evaluating partner loss (Sun et al., 2014). Over 75% of bonded male prairie voles maintain their bonds throughout life, and 80% never acquire new mates after the death of or abandonment by a female partner (Getz & Carter, 1996; Getz et al., 1993; Wang et al., 1997). Please keep in mind that in this study the little voles were separated from their partners for 4 weeks and were not physically hurt; however, the separation did psychologically affect the animals.

The temporary separation of male prairie voles from their partners significantly increased anxiety- and depression-like behaviors in the little animals. As a result, they did not seek out new partners. And even though pair-bonded voles usually respond aggressively toward unfamiliar females and intruder males, the voles that were separated from their partners were affiliative and lacked aggression. Physiological measures indicated that partner loss increased the density of various hormones in their bodies, which influenced their behaviors, and the separation had altered their neuropeptide systems (neuropeptides are small proteins produced by neurons that are responsible for synaptic transmissions) that disrupt bond-related behaviors. We could speculate that if they were human they were showing signs, based on their physiological responses, that they no longer cared much about their social roles. The researchers in this study concluded that partner loss in voles may resemble the neuro-biology that underlies partner loss and grief in humans who are strongly bonded to a partner. Although it is too much to expect someone should rush out and find a new partner, even if they could, finding other ways to positively attach—volunteering or getting an animal companion—can be soothing.

TO SUMMARIZE

The process of reactivating an image from explicit memory on the basis of its similarity to a current sensory cue or our present state of mind is called *ecphory* or an *ecphoric sensation*. Responses to our sense of smell, taste, touch, sight, or hearing involve memories of similar experiences, and they can elicit a variety of emotions, from sadness to nostalgia and even love. Our senses of smell and taste are the most common priming sources of what we remember, but loss-related memories may be activated through any of our senses. Everyday sensory experiences can trigger loss-related reminders. In loss, we may be affected by the absence of a loved one's smell, tasting a particular food, hearing a particular sound, missing the comfort of touch, or visually encountering something that reminds us of our loss. Intimate relationships can become internal regulators of our biological processes, and loss can result in biologic changes or medical conditions.

Research exploring partner loss in voles has provided us with some perspective about the attachment and loss, yet as humans we want relief from the anguish of grief as we take our memories with us to inform the present and future. Chapter 7 was written with the hope of providing further perspective about who we are in relation to our loss-related memories and how we can integrate memories of the people we loved and lost into our present lives.

Reflections

- What sensory memories do you have regarding a loved one who has passed away? Are there certain smells, tastes, sounds, or sights that evoke their memory?
- How have you altered mealtimes, holiday visits, or any routine activities you had with a departed loved one? What emotions and thoughts do these activities bring up in you now that the person who shared them with you has departed?
- Think about a photo that triggers positive memories that are also painful. What is your level of tolerance when looking at this photo? Has it changed over time?
- What are some of the ways in which you maintain physical and emotional security? Reaching out for social support, moving toward the establishment of new relationships, increasing connectedness with family members, physically moving, and searching for personal meaning are some of the ways mentioned in this chapter.

CHAPTER 7

ADAPTING TO LOSS

Growing up in the South, my husband reveled in country music, bluegrass, and gospel hymns. Every song seemed to tell a story, often with melancholic lyrics that were both dissonant and harmonious with the buoyant, hope-filled instrumentals. After he died, a person familiar to him professionally sent me a link to the gospel hymn "I'll Fly Away." Her choice likely reflected an awareness that my husband had been a military flight surgeon and private pilot, yet one of his greatest pleasures was sky gazing, any time of the day or night. Occasionally I would sit with him as he pointed out birds, dragonflies, bats, satellites, constellations, and ascending jets from the nearby Air Force base. One evening, as I walked through the doorway to join him, he seemed absorbed in the vast beyond. But when I reached him I realized he was flying away:

> *Some glad morning when this life is over*
> *I'll fly away*
> *To a home on God's celestial shore*
> *I'll fly away*
> *I'll fly away, oh, Glory*
> *I'll fly away*
> *When I die, Hallelujah, by and by*
> *I'll fly away.* (Brumley, 1932)

> **Rather than getting over, recovering from, or achieving closure to loss, we adapt to it. Memory is an adaptive process that enables us to use the past to imagine new possibilities.**

Rather than getting over, recovering from, or achieving closure to loss, we adapt to it. Memory is an adaptive process that enables us to use the past to imagine new possibilities. The aftermath of loss involves integrating memories of someone's presence with the reality of their absence. We rely on memories to continue our relationship with loved ones and to extend their presence within us into the future. This integration also involves adjusting our identity to changed circumstances. We may also grow into new personal roles and find new meanings in life, along with any meaning we derive from loss. Renowned psychoanalyst and philosopher Robert Stolorow believes the term "recovery" is a misnomer for those who have suffered a loss, given that human finitude is not an illness from which one can or should recover (Stolorow, 2011). The integration of the shattered world we once knew with an expanded emotional world depends, he believes, on the extent to which pain finds a relational home in which it can be held. Such is the challenge of people who encounter a significant loss: finding a place where grief can be understood, where longing can rest.

> **The challenge of people who encounter a significant loss is finding a place where grief can be understood, where longing can rest.**

Poet David Whyte (2015) provided direction for our feelings about a loss in his prose poem "Heartbreak":

> If heartbreak is inevitable and inescapable, it might be asking us to look for it and make friends with it, to see it as our constant and instructive companion, and even perhaps, in the depth of its impact as well as in its hindsight, to see it as its own reward. (pp. 101–106)

This chapter offers a perspective on adapting to loss. A few more concepts about memory will help explain why we struggle with the changes that occur when a loved one dies. Because grief is a personal melody, I "sing" in generalities about living alongside grief, and perhaps eventually beyond it, and I include some perspectives on our relationship with loss.

ALIGNING PRESENT AND PAST

In the early weeks and months after a loss, a loved one's death seems unreal, impossible to accept as we struggle to integrate the life we once knew into a life without them. A loved one's death seems so unreal because it does not fit into our existing framework of memories that continue to verify the person's presence. I am gradually not expecting to see my husband in all the usual places I used to find him, such as reading in his favorite chair or watching birds dart in and out of the fountain. Nevertheless, through thoughts, my memories often re-create his presence: The day after he died. I wondered if the hummingbird outside my window was him saying goodbye; I imagined together enjoying the numerous blooming agapanthus; also, I was annoyed at him for leaving so much junk in the garage.

> **A person's death is a distinct but incongruent memory, and it is hard to assimilate it into what we know and remember.**

Memory requires time to adjust to new and conflicting information. We form new associations, create new memories, and gain perspective on old memories through situations we encounter over time. Yet a person's death is a distinct but incongruent memory, and it is hard to assimilate it into what we know and remember. This incongruent information stands out—it demands our attention.

Isolation Effects

Our prior knowledge typically facilitates the processing of new information. The loss of a loved one is an interesting exception to this typical processing. We are more likely to remember events that are distinctively different from our memories because of something called an *isolation effect* or the *von Restorff effect* (Köhler & von Restorff, 1937). This effect can be applied to the loss of a loved one. Our preexisting memories of that person as present interfere with our processing the reality of their death, so we may struggle to integrate the information. The discrepancy between memories and present reality can activate distress, anguish, or the other emotions that define the experience of grief. As a simple example, after losing my husband, whenever I would open the freezer my attention would be drawn to his favorite food. It was a stimulus that activated memories, sadness, and a sense of incongruence that he was not here.

Memories associated with loss are subject to the fate of all of our memories; namely, if we do not constantly replay memories in our mind, they seem to fade beneath the layers of all the memories that follow, unless a present retrieval cue prompts their recall. The intensity of our response to repeated activation of a memory also eventually fades. In this sense, we become accustomed to what activates a memory and to the memory itself. Whereas early on, a particular memory trigger can make us weep, much later we may merely wince in distress. Overall, the passage of time enables loss-related memories to more easily rest alongside our other memories. Nevertheless, given the emotional intensity of a loss, the numerous ways we can remember, and the various situations that give rise to memories, there are times when we may be flooded with reminders and thus overcome with distress.

Congruency Effects

If grief results from the discrepancy between our memories of a loved one when they were alive and their absence through death, how can our brain process this difference in a way that does not result in intense emotion? So far, the fields of psychological and cognitive neuroscience have offered only limited understanding of how the brain assimilates new information with stored knowledge and beliefs about the world (Brod et al., 2013). Researchers have studied what is referred to as the *congruency effect*, which shows that qualitative features of information that are congruent with our memories are more effectively integrated into our memory network (Craik & Tulving, 1975; Staresina et al., 2009). For example, Mateo's wife battled a degenerative disease for several years. Although he desperately wanted to keep her with him, she deteriorated to the point where he considered, with guilt, the relief he might feel when she died. We could assume that when her expected death came, the loss was more congruent with his memories of gradually losing her during her illness. Nevertheless, we have to keep in mind that our responses to loss are personal and complex. In Mateo's case, several other factors produced an intense grief response to her loss. We cannot assume that people respond with less grief (or even relief) when the circumstances of death are prolonged or the loss is expected.

147

> The passage of time after a loss is helpful to us as the discrepancy between past and present memories becomes less stark.

Initially, of course, the death of a loved one is not at all congruent with our memories of them when they were living. Anything that reminds us of an enjoyable moment with the deceased can evoke anguish. Eventually, as that person's absence becomes more present in our memories, current situations without them align with the recent past. Thus, the passage of time beyond a loss is indeed helpful to us because the discrepancy between past and present memories becomes less stark.

Time

The passage of time has the potential to change how we feel about anything, of course. We learn and adapt as we incorporate new memories into preexisting memories. In response to a blog post about grief, people who have written me have shown through their comments that the passage of time has affected their responses to loss. For example, one person, who referred to herself as a recent widow wrote, "I am learning it just takes time to adapt, accept, forgive yourself, be angry, and cry Every day it gets better if you take time to let in life, the morning sun, the singing bird, anything of beauty."

Someone who lost her husband, father, and daughter stated:

I lost my daughter in 1985; do you get over it? No, you learn to live with it. I think of her nearly every day, but not as often as I did. . . . It takes however long it takes. You even finally see the brightness of the world, which is so beautiful.

Awaiting the passage of time, another person commented:

> It took me 10 years to adjust after my daughter died. Then my
> mother died shortly after. I have had to do a lot of adjusting just
> to remain upright. It is possible to do so. I have done it before
> but just now at my age it is harder to find the lost path. . . .
> I only hope for a little sanity in the future.

Commenting on the loss of a partner, a reader wrote:

> You have two choices when you lean forward: Fall or take a
> step. I prefer to take a step. I have been keeping this up . . . and
> slowly I see a difference. I am in the process of trying to find a
> new normal in my life. Not sure what will come of the changes
> I have been making, but it is at least moving forward.

> **We learn and adapt as we incorporate new memories into preexisting
> memories.**

Our recall of loss-related experiences may continue, although
our memory of the details of an experience with a deceased person
will fade over time. Ongoing experiences influence the gist of memories that are used to reconstruct details.[1] As we form new attachments and accumulate new experiences, the emotional impact of a
memory changes, much as a craving for something we have given
up may still exist in memory. We may, however, choose to hang onto

---

[1]Reconstruction may become distorted because the retrieval of memories
involves disparate brain areas (e.g., those that process vision and audition) that
were involved when the event was perceived.

the vividness of memories of a loved one because they hold a high value in our lives, and memories of them provide comfort and solace (Bonanno, 2010). Because the death of a loved one is incongruent with our present memory, the gradual obscuring of our memories about them may take many years. In some cases, a lifetime may not be long enough (O'Connor & McConnell, 2018).

FINDING A HOME FOR OUR STORY

Sharing autobiographical narratives of the deceased person with family members, friends, a therapist, a grief support group, or even strangers is believed to be a primary way to adapt our sense of identity after a loss (J. Baddeley & Singer, 2010; Kübler-Ross & Kessler, 2014; Neimeyer, 2001). Telling our grief-related story can help restore our sense of self. In situations where we are unafraid to convey our grief experiences, we become more free to move outside the domain of distress, where we can embrace the rest of what exists in our lives.

Telling stories about our painful experiences can have both psychological and physiological benefits (Pennebaker & Seagal, 1999; Woike & Matic, 2004). *Limbic resonance* refers to a mutual exchange whereby two humans become attuned to each other and internally adapt to each other's inner states (T. L. Lewis et al., 2000). As we broadcast information about our inner world, our stories about loss, expectations, and reactions echo themes that begin to give the listener a sense of what it feels like to live in our world (T. L. Lewis et al., 2000). The emotional resonance found in friendships, family relationships, or romantic partnerships is physiologically regulating; intimacy can steady a person whose emotions are tumbling out of control (T. L. Lewis et al., 2000). Putting into words what we feel can disrupt the brain's emotional responses, which would otherwise occur when negative emotional images are present (Lieberman et al., 2007). Moreover, the self-exploration involved in the narration of suffering enriches our lives and creates the potential for learning and insight (McAdams & Mclean, 2013).

We may not receive the support we need, however, but it is important to keep searching for it. For example, when Samantha's soul mate died, she felt misunderstood by others who did not seem receptive to her grief stories. After several months, her sister became frustrated by Samantha's grief and told her that it was time to "accept the loss and move on." Deciding to explore grief support groups, Samantha eventually found one in which she connected with someone who had endured similar circumstances. Likewise, a reader who responded to one of my blog posts mentioned the following:

> It's so hard when people don't understand that you don't just get over losing someone. I lost both my parents recently. I feel most comfortable with people who have had a similar loss. It helps when people understand how you feel.

Shared experiences give us the sense that we are not alone. Grief support groups can provide a place for our feelings and lessen a feeling of isolation. Still, if a particular group does not resonate, it is essential for a griever to try another, and another, until some emotional connection with other people is found. Responses to the loss of a relationship differ considerably among people. The dynamics of an attachment, the personal history each individual brought to the liaison, and numerous other factors make everyone's grief different. So many grief support groups are available, though, that it should be possible to find at least one person in one of them whose experiences echo our own.

Narrative Risk and the Silence of Grief

There is a double edge to grief stories: narrative risks. Conveying a narrative of losing someone important can relieve us, but it may also trigger grief. Describing a narrative about loss brings to the surface various episodic memories, emotional memories, and semantic memories (memories about knowledge and basic facts; Cabeza & St. Jacques, 2007). Our stories, and the self-awareness created by them, can help soothe a broken heart. We must be mindful, though, lest they plunge us, over and over, into despair.

> **Conveying a narrative of losing someone important can relieve us, but it may also trigger grief.**

We now have some contrary evidence (in the psychology literature, diverse opinions and conflicting research results are common) challenging the assumption that to achieve a successful and healthy recovery, grief-stricken individuals must talk about their grief (Cabeza & St. Jacques, 2007). Recent work on loss and bereavement has found that unspoken memory—the withholding of autobiographical memories about loss and the departed loved one—can preserve an existing identity, and not sharing can give us a sense of purpose in the face of grief (J. Baddeley & Singer, 2010). This suggests that we ought not view silence in response to loss as a form of denial. Unspoken memories can be sources of stability, growth, or resistance in response to the demand for change that loss seems to impose on us (J. Baddeley & Singer, 2010). Moreover, many people do not want others to perceive them only as someone whose grief has become tantamount to an identity.

Whether or not we talk or write about our grief, though, a significant part of heartache lingers within inexplicable implicit memories. These implicit memories create sensations we feel about the deceased, and they do not translate into the words we have for narrative memory; in fact, they can convey the pain of loss. For example, John wrote to me explaining how he feels that, internally, his loss could never be conveyed by his words: "I lost my dear son.... The breadth and depth of such a loss [are] inexpressible. He is with me every day."

The Pitfalls of Redemptive Stories and Emotional Avoidance (Dissociation)

Plenty of podcasts, videos, and books explain the experiences of those who make meaning from, discover a positive outcome of, or impart goodness from their tragedies. Creating a meaning or purpose comes from within each individual and, I believe, cannot be prescribed. In some cases, it's nearly impossible to achieve. For example, Daniella lost her twin children in a tragic automobile accident. She not only grieves their loss but also mourns the future they never had. She said, "Every time I see children who are the age they would be, I imagine what they would be like." When her memories are triggered, she takes a breath and tells her children she loves them and hopes they are safe, wherever they are.

> Turning loss into something meaningful may not align with who we are, the nature of our loss, or what is possible for us to do.

One difficulty for those who have lost a child involves what we naturally do with memory, that is, we mentally time travel into the future. Parents who have lost a child cannot help but project what the future might have been at any point in time for the dead children. They have many comparisons, such as the children of friends or relatives, who become markers for the age their child would have been and are reminders of the lost opportunities in a missing future of a deceased child. Turning loss into something meaningful may not align with who we are, the nature of our loss, or what is possible for us to do.

A perhaps-unfortunate cultural norm in Western society is a preference for *redemptive stories*, namely, when an experience is narrated in a way that communicates growth, meaning making, or resolution (McLean et al., 2020). This cultural norm—it may even be stronger, a directive—implies that narrators should not ruminate about distress and that they should provide satisfactory endings and redemptive meanings from suffering (McAdams & Mclean, 2013). We tend to applaud those who can regale us with stories in which the anguish of tragedy is tied up with a neat bow. Why? Because such stories make us feel good. In Western culture, redemptive stories are seen as reflecting the health of the storytellers and suggest that they have more adaptive personality traits (e.g., agreeableness, conscientiousness, and extraversion) compared with others who have less redemptive life stories (Guo et al., 2016).

Loss, like trauma, is not necessarily redeemable.

This cultural expectation has potential drawbacks. Loss, like trauma, is not necessarily redeemable. When people share stories that do not align with the listener's preference for trauma to be redeemed, they may feel unheard, isolated, or devalued, despite the fact that they need—and seek—support (Guo et al., 2016). For instance, Daniella, mentioned earlier, eventually found her way back into life after tragically losing her twins, but not without many years of encountering disappointment that people around her, including relatives, dismissed how she missed her children and did not acknowledge their birthdays or death days. She eventually became hesitant to share her grief. This may be but one example of the positive psychology movement gone awry: Happiness and positive emotion can be overvalued and those who mourn underappreciated.

It's easy to see why people in Western culture may silently hold their grief: If they do otherwise, they risk social isolation. Researchers have found that regulating negative emotions tends to foster a griever's connection to others, allowing them to gain support from others (Harber & Pennebaker, 1992). But because negative emotions can create discomfort or stress in the listener (at least in Western culture), emotions such as distress or anguish may limit potential support for the griever (Bonanno, 2012). Therefore, according to researchers, emotional avoidance and self-deceptive processes can be a way of successfully coping in the face of the pain of loss (Keltner & Bonanno, 1997). How sad!

For example, a study of marital loss in midlife found that smiling and genuine laughter in the bereaved while they discussed their deceased spouses resulted in better relationships with others and evoked compassion and the desire to comfort, as opposed to those who displayed only nongenuine or social laughter (Bonanno, 2012; Keltner & Bonanno, 1997). In Eastern cultures, where there tends to be a more dominant belief in the deceased's continued presence and a continuity between the living and the dead, the pressure to express positive emotions and "get over" one's grief is less prominent (Bonanno, 2012).

My Uncle Orazio, a masculine Sicilian, happened to be a good role model when discussing the departed. He tended to bring up dead people, such as my mother or his mother, even when they were not the conversation topic. With tremendous dignity, and with tears in his eyes, Uncle Orazio would recount a memory of what that person would have said, what they had done in a similar situation, or anything else about them that happened to come into his mind. Then he would comfortably move on to something else. The deceased and what they would have contributed to the discussion were part of the conversation. This allowed listeners—or me, at least—a sense of a loved one's presence, the ways they thought or felt, despite their absence.

Unfortunately, people who express sadness often encounter a negative response, either because someone tries to "make them happy," changes the subject, or just shrinks away. Rightly or wrongly, grievers can come to expect such a response. A reader of my blog posts, whose 24-year-old son died in his sleep, wrote, "The grief stabs me in my heart when I least expect it. It is debilitating and most people just don't understand, or want to be around when I'm dishing out. I get it."

> **If we collude with the notion that we should "smile and be happy" when we feel otherwise, we may wonder who among our friends and acquaintances can truly empathize with us.**

Some grievers describe their understandable intolerance of prolonged social situations because they fear losing control of their feelings, being unable to convey a favorable impression, or believing that other people will negatively view their expressions of authentic grief (Clark & Wells, 1995; K. V. Smith & Ehlers, 2021). A study of social disconnection after bereavement found that emotional suppression and self-monitoring are associated with higher psychological distress, an altered sense of self in social situations, and cognitive demands necessary to suppress grief. One of my bereaved clients told me that, during social gatherings, if something or someone activated a grief-related memory, she would talk about it, often announcing,

"I'm going to cry." Then she would continue her story while crying and move on to the next subject. Uncle Orazio would have been proud of her. Thus, if a griever's social network is perceived as emotionally receptive, compassionate, and able to tolerate distress, the griever's social fears and the associated consequences of social disconnection may not be so prominent (K. V. Smith et al., 2020). If we collude with the notion that we should "smile and be happy" when we feel otherwise, we may wonder who among our friends and acquaintances can truly empathize with us.

Even unshared joy can encumber us.

Even unshared joy can encumber us. Those who grieve miss sharing joyful moments with the loved one who died, and friends and relatives of mourners may feel similarly about the comparative absence of the once-joyful person who is now grieving. Granted, mourners do not always consider the impact of their sadness on others. A parent who mourns the loss of a spouse may be unaware that their children, extended family members, and friends miss the parent's ebullient self. Anyone who is grieving the loss of a loved one may innocently neglect the impact of their inner retreat on friends and relatives. The people who remain in our lives may become frustrated and want us to get over the loss and reengage with life as we knew it in part because they miss us—the person they have known differently. Moreover, through emotional contagion they may experience what the griever feels. As a result, sharing touchy or tearful conversations about the deceased in Western culture is often avoided in the interest of rekindling upbeat friendships, despite the fact that the "downbeat" stories may genuinely help the grieving person. We live in a culture that seems to overvalue happiness and pleasure. It is no wonder, then, that we have trouble indulging in grief.

The Erroneous Pursuit of Happiness

Numerous self-help books will tell you exactly what to do, how to do it, and how often to do something to get over grief and find happiness, but happiness, in and of itself, can be an elusive goal. One reader of my blog mused about striving for happiness: "So long as there is a promise that it might disappear, you continually strive for that and will always feel like a failure. When you learn to accept the pain as normal and ongoing, you may find some peace." Another pointedly stated:

> Articles that tell you that you will "grow" after loss or that list three dozen ways to "overcome" your grief are actually insulting and hurtful. I don't want to grow, become stronger or move on. I'd rather be weak and have my child back.

Indeed, researchers have found that valuing happiness might be self-defeating because the more we value it, the more likely we are to experience disappointment when we are not happy (Mauss et al., 2012). In essence, people who highly value happiness may set standards that are hard to achieve, and when people cannot meet the standards they have set for themselves they are bound to be disappointed (Mauss et al., 2012). Thus, in the case of wanting happiness, researchers have concluded that people may feel worse off the more they want it, and that overvaluing this positive emotional state can lead you to be less happy, even if it is within your reach. Similarly, if grievers believe they can just "get over it" and be happy, they are more likely to be miserable. Instead of seeking happiness or a resolution to grief, finding new meaning in life, or even meaning regarding the loss itself (if possible), may be a more adaptive response to a significant loss.

Uplifting emotions, such as joy or excitement, are considered positive and are associated with individual success, good health, and high self-esteem, primarily in Western culture. Although Westerners may assume that all people should strive to experience more positive emotions in their lives, this is not always the case in other cultures. For example, in many Asian cultural contexts happiness may be associated with negative social consequences, such as jealousy in others (Leu et al., 2011). In cultures informed by the Buddhist belief that pure pleasantness is impossible to attain or can lead to suffering (Leu et al., 2011), the goal may be a moderation of positive emotion, instead of a maximization. Therefore, balancing positive and negative emotions may be a cultural goal in Asian contexts, such as Japan, China, or Thailand, but in the United States maximizing positive emotions may be a greater cultural goal. As a result, grief is seen as something to be avoided.

The positive psychology movement began in 1998 as an attempt to turn away from psychopathology and toward what can go *right* with people. It focused on positive subjective experiences, positive individual characteristics, and factors that contribute to the flourishing of people and groups (Gable & Haidt, 2005; Peterson & Park, 2003; Seligman & Csikszentmihalyi, 2000). Researchers found that positive experiences and a concentration on optimal functioning boosted well-being when participants were informed about a happiness intervention, endorsed it, and were committed to it. Thus happiness, the theory goes, requires effort along with belief (Lyubomirsky et al., 2011). For example, research regarding what makes people happier has pointed to such things as practicing optimistic thinking by visualizing your best possible future self and expressing gratitude through writing (Lyubomirsky et al., 2011). However, being told that a certain activity can make you happier is also subject to a placebo effect; namely, if we believe something can make us happier, then the possibility exists that, at least temporarily, it will.

> **Grief tells us an unhappy truth we may rather not know, but it does not tell us to be miserable in every aspect of our lives.**

Activating any emotion that has a mood-elevating quality will lead to momentary happiness, if not long-term content. Keep in mind, though, that the quest for experiencing happy emotions may be overrated. All emotions, both positive and negative ones, have played an important role in our evolution and survival. The emotions that create grief tell us that we are missing someone highly valued in our lives. Grief tells us an unhappy truth we may rather not know, but it does not tell us to be miserable in every aspect of our lives.

RESILIENCE

> **An expectation that people can find positive meaning in adverse circumstances or profit when faced with stress, trauma, or forms of adversity may, at times, be misleading.**

Similar to redemptive stories, the popular concept of *resilience* refers to some people's ability to respond to hardship positively, to spring back or not be sunk by difficulties, and to trust in a better future. Resilience is associated with cognitive and personality factors that allow people to seek positive meaning during trying circumstances or to imbue ordinary events with a positive meaning (Tugade & Fredrickson, 2004). A resilient person may be able to give stronger weight to optimistic interpretations and not focus on pessimistic ones. Given my own personal history, some mental health professionals or grief researchers may claim that resilience enabled me to find my way past the losses I experienced. But was it? If resilience has anything to do with bringing the deceased with us into the future—our continued bonds with loved ones we have lost—then I might agree. In retrospect, I believe I eventually bounced back into life because I brought my loved ones with me through my memories of them. Resilience and continuing bonds are very separate concepts, though; moreover, for several years after the loss of my mother I would hardly describe myself as resilient, given how I felt and how I performed in school! Even so, others may have assumed I had resilience. The expectation that people can find positive meaning in adverse circumstances, or profit when faced with stress, trauma, or forms of adversity, may at times be misleading. Such expectations can lead us to believe we are defective if internally we are aware that we do not follow that course given the negative emotions we feel while stepping forward.

> Labeling emotions as positive or negative has little to do with their value but instead involves how they motivate us by the way they make us feel. Like all emotions, sadness, despite how it makes us feel, is simply trying to inform and protect us.

As you consider the concept of resilience, keep in mind that we may not like feeling some of our negative emotions, but they serve an important purpose: They inform us. Labeling emotions as positive or negative has little to do with their value but instead involves how they motivate us by the way they make us feel. Negative emotions like distress, fear, anger, disgust, and shame motivate us to do something to avoid experiencing them, or they urge us to behave in ways that will relieve their effects. For example, we are motivated to retreat from a dangerous situation on the basis of our fear, or we seek comfort to relieve distress. Sadness (distress) is a negative emotion that helps us to remember, rather than forget, what it is or was that we desired. After a loss, sadness promotes personal reflection that is important to us and turns our attention inward to promote acceptance (Lazarus, 1991). Thus, sadness allows us to consider the impact of our loss and the necessity of revising our objectives and strategies for the future. Like all emotions, sadness, despite how it makes us feel, is simply trying to inform and protect us. If we show preference to the concept of resilience, or apply an optimistic gloss to negative emotions, then instead of backing off from a dangerous situation or seeking comfort for our distress we might instead disconnect ourselves from our thoughts, feelings, and surroundings. This, in turn, might endanger or deprive us in the long term.

According to researchers, resilient people have a greater tendency to draw on positive emotions in times of stress and use them to their advantage, and therefore they may have a better capacity to learn from life's setbacks than less resilient people (e.g., Feldman Barrett et al., 2001; Salovey et al., 1999). However, we can learn from any emotion we experience. Psychiatrist Donald L. Nathanson, who has devoted much of his career to the study of emotions, in particular, shame, explained that shame is a teacher because it draws us within ourselves to think deeply about the self (Nathanson, 1992).

In response to loss, resilience is considered to be a trait that involves a capacity for generative experiences and positive emotions while maintaining relatively stable and healthy physical and psychological functioning (Bonanno, 2005, 2010; Bonanno & Keltner, 1997; Bonanno et al., 2002; Keltner & Bonanno, 1997; Tugade & Fredrickson, 2004). Regardless of the level of distress or perceived health, resilient individuals are thought to demonstrate a capacity for *affective complexity*: the ability to experience positive and negative emotions relatively independently (Bonanno, 2010). Even so, researchers interested in the impact of adversity on resilience have found that higher resilience is often the result of having overcome some lifetime adversity (or a history of adversities). Having had an easy path does not necessarily build resilience; neither does having only a history of high adversity without the experience of overcoming hardships (Seery, 2011).

The concept of resilience introduces the possibility that emotional challenges enhance the ability to rebound and that flexibility fosters positive functioning. Those who experience enduring hardship may become resourceful and develop a greater sense of agency, rather than become passive victims who only suffer as a result (Daly, 2020; Frost & Hoggett, 2008). The use of adaptive coping strategies, including the pursuit of meaningful activities, reaching out to others for support, taking action to improve a situation, or viewing a challenging condition more positively have been promoted by mental health professionals as a means to increase resilience in people (Feder et al., 2016). Such cognitive approaches, which involve reframing an experience, diverting attention away from it, or finding support around it, may work in some situations and for some people. A similar, yet extreme, rationalization for hardship is the adage "What doesn't kill you makes you stronger."

When emotions occur in persistent or repeated forms, we consider them dispositional characteristics of the individual; we attribute the emotions to that person's psychological makeup. As a result, we tend to use the language of *personality traits* rather than the language of *emotional states* to define a person (Plutchik, 2000). In this regard, we may characterize an individual as resilient, narcissistic, or neurotic, or use another term that reflects a particular trait. Describing people in terms of a personality trait may be confusing, however, because it obscures the emotions that motivate their behavior and their memories of emotional experiences that script their responses to life's hardships.

Although resilience is considered a personality trait, or an attitude by which one approaches difficult situations, it is a multidimensional construct (Southwick & Charney, 2012). Multiple interacting factors are assumed to play critical roles in developing resilience, including genetic, developmental, psychosocial, neurochemical, functional neural circuitry, and other selective individual-difference variables (M. C. Davis et al., 2004; Wu et al., 2013; Zautra et al., 2005). Just because a person does or does not bounce back into life after experiencing a loss does not mean they are or are not resilient. The loss of a soul mate is often a circumstance from which people have difficulty bouncing back. We adapt differently depending on numerous other significant factors, especially those that involve our relationship with the person we have lost.

Episodic memory is instrumental in producing thoughts for the future; it helps us dream, plan, and have hope. We learn from both the minuscule and the enormous challenges we encounter in life, and "hope" means that we can respond to negative emotions by projecting what we learn onto an anticipated future. Hope represents a trust in the fact that good feelings are possible, despite the present impediments to them. In Chapter 8, we look at some of the ways we continue learning from loved ones who have died and the role of hope in adapting to loss.

TO SUMMARIZE

We adapt to loss rather than get over it. The notion of not accepting a loss implies that the bereaved person is consciously resisting the reality of a loved one's death when in fact a loved one's death may seem unreal or impossible to accept because it does not fit into one's existing framework of memories that continue to verify the person's presence. Our memory requires time to adjust to new and conflicting information. The intensity of our response to memories fades with their repeated activation, as do the details of experiences with a now-deceased person. Initially, though, reminders of enjoyable moments with someone who has died can activate anguish. Narrating our grief-related stories can be relieving but may also trigger grief; however, some research suggests that it is unnecessary for grief-stricken individuals to talk about their grief in order to adapt, and unspoken memory can preserve and existing identity.

A norm in Western culture implies that people who provide satisfactory endings and redemptive means from suffering are more widely accepted. Resilience is associated with cognitive and personality factors that allow people to seek positive meaning during trying circumstances. In Eastern cultures, a belief in the deceased's continued presence and a continuity between the living and the dead is more prominent than in Western culture. Given that we live in a culture that seems to overvalue pleasure and happiness, we are likely to be disappointed when we are not happy. Although we may not like feeling some of our negative emotions, they serve an important purpose: to inform us. Labeling emotions "positive" or "negative" has little to do with their value but instead involves how they motivate us through how they make us feel.

Reflections

- How has it been helpful or hurtful to share your grief-related stories with others? In what ways are you inhibited about sharing what you feel? What kinds of responses have you encountered in social gatherings if you bring up your loss?
- Consider the coping strategies you have used in response to loss. Do any of your strategies result in new learning that may help you? Do any of them hinder you?

CHAPTER 8

LOSING AND REDISCOVERING OURSELVES

A jar of dried fava beans from my mother's last crop perched on my father's workshop shelf for 10 years. The cambered mahogany beans were among the few of my father's possessions that I took home after he died. Decades later, I learned that fava beans hold great significance for Sicilians. During the Middle Ages, a drought had destroyed crops in Sicily. St. Joseph answered the prayers of the people for rain, and the surviving plants, saving them from famine, were fava beans (Eplett, 2012). The Feast of St. Joseph is celebrated by Sicilian people on March 19th with table and altar adornments featuring dried fava beans. They are a symbol of hope when spirits are low and a token of luck for those who carry one with them. The jar of fava beans has lived on my bookshelf for 50 years, and now, of course, I keep one of them with me.

Who or what is actually "lost" when we experience the death of someone significant in our lives? In one sense, we may become "lost" ourselves when we lose someone dear to us. In this final chapter, we take a look at emotions, thoughts, and memories that create the sense of losing oneself through loss. Those who perceive death as final in terms of a relationship with a loved one do not believe that positive feelings will be available again. Hope, though, is a sense of trust that good feelings are still there, through the continuing bonds that exist within our memories. Thus, in this chapter, we explore how hope uses our memories to help us recover our identity and self-definition and maintain an internal relationship with a loved one.

BECOMING LOST IN LOSS

Just as Polaris—the North Star—is a fixed destination in the northern sky, a guiding directional light for navigators and a metaphorical beacon of hope, relationships are also an anchor or watchtower that keep us from getting lost amid the changes that happen in life. The awareness that someone is missing outside of our being corresponds to their absence within us that has contributed to our self-definition. Along with loss, our identity no longer exists in relation to a familiar living being, even though our continued bonds with them may keep them with us.

When we are lost in response to loss we may not know which way to go, where to turn, or what to do. We may feel vulnerable, exposed, or alone. We may yearn for the times when our path and our identity seemed more defined. As I became aware of my disorientation after my husband's death, I recalled flying in a light aircraft across the country with him 40 years ago. I obviously considered him a trustworthy pilot and had an illusion of safety regarding the plane itself. Nightfall was upon us as we were crossing the huge expanse of Lake Michigan. Suddenly, the gyroscope—a motion sensor, compass, and turn coordinator that detects changes in orientation—malfunctioned. As light was leaving the sky, and without a working gyroscope, we had little idea of the plane's orientation relative to the horizon, and being over water made it nearly impossible to gauge our position. We became hypervigilant. Fortunately, we eventually landed safely at an airport across the lake.

When we are vulnerable or lost we may not know what to do or where to turn, yet our emotions make us pay attention. They can help us adapt to changed, threatening, or unusual circumstances. Memory will remind us of any similar situations we have experienced throughout our lives, and we can use its ability to project into the future in order to plan and anticipate our next steps. Many of my clients and friends have described how a loss resulted in their indecisiveness, confusion, and a general sense of being adrift. Accepting the shame of not knowing what to do when we are lost can help us maintain our attention and keep moving in a healthy direction. This is echoed in the words of the poet David Whyte (2015), who wrote:

> Not knowing what to do is just as real and just as useful as knowing what to do. Not knowing stops us from taking false directions.
> Not knowing what to do, we start to pay real attention. Just as people lost in the wilderness, on the cliff face or in a blizzard pay attention with a kind of acuity that they would not have if they thought they knew where they were. Why? Because for those who are really lost, their life depends on paying real attention. If you think you know where you are, you stop looking. (p. 131)

Relationships are built on memories that are infused with emotion and imagery.

Take a moment and imagine someone close to you who has died. Without naming or explaining what you feel, focus on the sensations inside of you. Our implicit memories give the deceased a presence through the bodily sensations we experience. Implicit memories of a loved one exist inside of us along with our explicit memories of moments with them that we consciously recall when a present stimulus evokes them. We do not have to relinquish our attachments and, even if we could, how would we? Relationships are built on memories that are infused with emotion and imagery. We cannot erase memories, although it is possible to pay less attention when they are activated or avoid situations that trigger them.

The night before my husband's stroke, we went grocery shopping late in the evening—a silly ritual we have had throughout our marriage. A month later, I went to that specific store again; however, I went at midday, intentionally avoiding the evening, which likely would remind me of our last outing together. As I hurried through the aisles, various images of being there with him, along with the sensations I felt, made me aware of his absence, which conflicted with memories of his presence. At the same time, I also sensed a mental cloudiness and a numbness that stood guard at the gate to my feelings. I felt somewhat lost. Once I was safely at home, I was able to experience my sadness and cry, acknowledging the reminders of positive memories that led me to miss him.

Losing ourselves in images and sensations that create a momentary unreality are sometimes described as "creepy" experiences after a loss. I remember plenty of creepy moments after each of my parents died, sensing their presence in various ways, but I didn't expect to have such experiences after the loss of my husband. In one instance, a soulful friend from a Latin American culture asked if my husband's spirit was able to leave. He explained that his mother, who had died when he was a child, had remained in the house for many years, making noises that alerted the family to her presence. His father had beseeched her to go, assuring her that they would be okay.

A sense of someone's presence is influenced by memories that are colored by our sociocultural history, our personal emotional need to keep them near, and our awareness that a loved one would have been reluctant to go. Are the deceased unable to find their way, or are we so lost in the shadow of grief that we keep them near? Given what my friend had conveyed, and perhaps even if he had not told me his story, my own superstitions and eerie feelings arose when the alarm sensors on the bedroom windows suddenly failed to work one day. Was my husband hanging around and reluctant to go? For a moment, I felt lost without him at home to attend to the problem. Having to problem-solve on my own, I decided that two alarm sensor batteries needed to be changed but, adding fuel to my superstitious imaginings, the sensors still did not work once the new batteries were installed. Although I did not remember doing so, I had inadvertently switched off the sensors on the windows; however, the thoughts I attributed to my feelings kept my husband around at a time when I felt somewhat lost without him.

The complexity of adapting to changed circumstances may lead to a sense of being lost in indecision about things that do not necessarily need to be decided at the time, such as whether we should remain in our home or move, whether we should give away a loved one's possessions or keep them, or whether we should take a trip alone or stay home. Creating more change may be our attempt to achieve resolution or avoid familiar situations that activate distress. Change may help some of us in our efforts to restore ourselves, yet for others it may be further disorienting.

> **Acceptance is a recognition that, despite our losses and feeling lost, we still have the power to be safe, to control, to problem-solve, to participate in life, and to partake in giving.**

The sense of being lost may also result from the changed meanings in our lives. The meanings have changed implicitly. Implicit meanings are those that we feel but for which we do not have words. We sense the meanings in our body. For example, the meaning of watching a baseball game has changed since my husband died. I can feel it, but not articulate it. The simple things we shared with another person, where the meaning has changed without their presence, can affect us in profound ways.

Acceptance of loss is not resignation motivated by distress or anguish; it is a compassionate recognition that we have these feelings. Acceptance is a recognition that, despite our losses and feeling lost, we still have the power to be safe, to control, to problem-solve, to participate in life, and to partake in giving. We can perceive our feelings, live them, and accept them as an indication of what is happening now.

Time certainly enables us to reconcile the present with the contents of our memories. We eventually become more familiar with someone's absence, and our memories adapt to the reality of loss, even though we may use our memories to continue a bond with the departed. Through memory we can also project images into our future: We can hope.

TRYING ON HOPE

We learn from both the minuscule and the enormous challenges we encounter, and we can respond to painful emotions by projecting what we have previously learned onto our expectations of what lies ahead. Episodic memory is forward looking and instrumental in that it produces images and thoughts for the future, helping us dream, plan, and anticipate the future on the basis of knowledge from the past (Schacter et al., 2012). In fact, a primary and adaptive function of memory is that it provides a foundation to predict or simulate the future (Boyer, 2008; Schacter & Addis, 2007).

Hope does not technically fit the criteria for an emotion, although researchers have referred to it as an "emotional state" (Schacter et al., 2012). Nevertheless, its importance for human survival has led some researchers to consider it a basic emotion that involves responses such as goal setting, investment in change, and coping (Bruininks & Malle, 2005). Perhaps hope is better understood as a cognition (thought) that involves expectations about a possible future good that creates a certain mood (a prolonged emotional state). Although hope lacks the immediacy and intensity of reflexive emotions, it can shape one's outlook on life on the basis of memories of previous experiences. Hope involves mental time travel that can structure our lives in anticipation of the future, influence our present state of mind, and alter behaviors. The cognitions associated with hope—how we think when we are hopeful—create expectations that are pathways to desired goals and create the will to pursue them (Snyder, Harris, et al., 1991). Hope protects us from external threats or inner vulnerabilities. As such, the role of hope has been explored as a coping resource against despair (Lazarus, 1999). Hopelessness, however, and the inability to give up a useless hope, are associated with depression and anxiety (Abramson et al., 1989; Nesse, 1999; Starr & Davila, 2012).

Hope as Distinct From Optimism

Hope and optimism have often been linked as similar psychological states, even though they have significant differences (e.g., Maier et al., 2000; Peterson & Seligman, 2004).[1] Researchers distinguish the concepts on the basis of the expectation of outcome; that is, optimism reflects greater certainty in an outcome and hope is related to more uncertainty but involves higher personal importance, commitment, and confidence in terms of the subjective probability that we may realize a positive future (Bruininks & Malle, 2005; Gasper et al., 2020). Hope involves determination to pursue goal-directed behavior and involves the pathways to meet those goals.

---

[1]For example, Schacter et al. (2012) pointed to studies establishing that views of the future are associated with a prevalent positivity or optimism bias.

Hoping is generally considered more specific than being optimistic and involves more of an investment of energy and personal control even when the odds are not in one's favor (Bruininks & Malle, 2005). The probability of attainment has to be realistic, what we hope for has to be personally or socially acceptable, the outcome or event has to be perceived as important, and the hopeful person should be willing to take action (if possible) to achieve their goal (Bruininks & Malle, 2005). Therefore, hope can contribute to our health and well-being if we have the motivation to remain engaged with a future outcome and are able to anticipate how to reach that outcome (Krafft et al., 2020).

Memory and Hope

As a subset of episodic memory, *prospective memory* is at work whenever we recall something we had intended to do at a future point or when we generate a specific purpose that must be delayed (Gardner & Ascoli, 2015). Prospective memory aligns with hope as a pathway for our thoughts about the future, providing a sense of agency and motivating us to consider alternative routes to reach our goals (Snyder, Irving, & Anderson, 1991). Although some of our planning maps out a tangible goal—such as a trip to visit old college friends to distract ourselves from reminders of loss—we may also use imagery in a hopeful way, planning for a more desirable future. We experience hope (or despair) in the midst of our long-term efforts (Nesse, 1999).

A particular experience in my life involving two loving uncles (and the early loss of one of them) later provided a sense of agency and hope that I could change a future circumstance or even a sociocultural bias that might hold me back. The experience also contributed to my hope for a special relationship in my life with someone who resonated with my interests. As a 13-year-old, before the women's liberation movement took hold in the United States, I began working on weekends for my Uncle Frank, who was partnered with my Uncle Orazio at their auto-wrecking yard. Along with selling parts from wrecked cars, they also sold new and rebuilt parts. I earned money fetching needed parts for Uncle Frank on the shelves of the aisles behind the counter: sparkplugs, rotors, fan belts, hoses, brake shoes, clamps, voltage regulators, fuel pumps, carburetors, and gaskets, among other things. By the time I was 15, I was often behind the counter alone when Uncle Frank was helping Uncle Orazio out in the yard. In the early 1960s, all of the patrons were male, and I didn't take it personally when they doubted a young female could accurately look up and sell them the parts they needed. Often they would wait around until Uncle Frank returned from the yard, wanting verification that the item I sold them was correct. Upon looking up the part number he always nonchalantly said, "Yes, she's right."

When I was 19, I visited Uncle Frank in the hospital as he was dying from Hodgkin's disease. Within the walls of that room he seemed lonesome, connected only to tubes entering his body from surrounding devices. Uncle Frank couldn't talk, but he could nod, and I knew he understood me. I explained how much I appreciated his belief in me as a young girl, trusting that I could learn about how cars worked and that I could sell their parts. Proudly, I described how I had successfully changed the water pump on my car when it had frozen up. Tears filled his eyes. I kissed him, told him I loved him, and then left, because I have never liked hospitals.

I always had hope that somehow my mother and all the others I have loved and lost would help me find what I needed in my adult life. As discussed in Chapter 2, implicit (unconscious) memories influence our attraction to certain people. Numerous work and life experiences, including graduate training in psychology, muted the memories of my little job at the wrecking yard. Nonetheless, selling auto parts gave me plenty of knowledge (semantic memories) to impress a guy who loved fast and exotic automobiles. My husband liked telling the story of our first date when, in stiletto heels, I offered to either push his temperamental Alfa Romeo or pop the clutch to activate the dead battery. My love for my uncles, and their belief in me as a young girl who could learn the basics of automobile mechanics, was buried in my mind, yet it seemed to emerge in my attraction to the man I later married. It didn't take the women's liberation movement to help me believe in myself, but it did take relationships with adults who respected my competence. We continue to learn from those who have contributed to our identity, long after losing them.

> **Having hope means we can learn from both the minuscule and the enormous challenges that we encounter in life; it means that we can respond to negative emotions by projecting what we learn onto an anticipated future that holds meaning.**

Learning From Hope

Hope does not mean we necessarily face loss with positive feelings. It means we can learn from both the minuscule and the enormous challenges we encounter in life; it means we can respond to negative emotions by projecting what we learn onto an anticipated future that holds meaning for us. When we are coping with loss and feeling lost, recognizing that memories of the deceased can guide us will actually shape how we traverse the current situation and can give us hope. For example, a graduate student asked for my advice about potential dissertation topics. The student revealed that she was grappling with the sudden and traumatic loss of her sister the year before. I suggested that, if it was emotionally possible for her to do so, she might consider researching the subject of sibling loss, adding, "And your sister will be with you." The student's dissertation was an excellent research study that explored the continuing bonds with siblings after their death (M. S. F. Anderson, 2020). Her memories of her sister enabled her to find a path to reach her desired goals, and I am certain her sister will always be part of her hopes.

Hope doesn't extinguish grief but, with help from our memories, it can take our loss with us to better, or different, future places.

Humans adapt differently, and the capacity to learn enables us to have hope that we will get through a tough time, even if that hope is merely a glimmer. Hope does not extinguish grief, but it can take our memories of those we have lost with us to better or different future places. If our purpose is to hide or protect our sense of self, that self, that image of who we are that at the moment seems lost, does not learn from the loss. Negative emotions may enter into our consciousness, and they may hurt. Imagining our inner pain as fatal results in distress, anger, fear, or shame—and leads us to erroneously believe ourselves or our lives are defective. In these ways, we obstruct the possibility of learning from negative emotions that, just like positive ones, inform who we are and motivate us to be even more who we are.

Certainly, this last chapter would have been a perfect place to write something that could erase the grief of those who suffer from it. By now, though, you know that grief isn't something to get over. My goal instead in these chapters was to offer psychological insights that might help you make sense of the grieving process and more deeply understand what you are going through. Like the symbolism around the cherished fava beans in the jar on my shelf, I leave you with hope.

TO SUMMARIZE

We may experience a sense of being lost ourselves when faced with a significant loss. Relationships are like a guiding force amid the changes that happen in life. Thus, our path, identity, and self-definition may be questioned; however, emotions make us pay attention to changed conditions and help us adapt to changed, unusual, or threatening circumstances.

Implicit memories give the deceased a presence through the bodily sensations we experience. Implicit memories of a loved one exist inside of us along with our explicit memories of moments with them that we consciously recall when a present stimulus evokes them. We may experience a sense of a loved one's presence that is influenced by our cultural history, emotional needs, and empathy with the assumed reluctance to leave us on the part of the person who has died. Acceptance of loss is a recognition that we have these feelings yet also have the power to be safe and engage in life.

Episodic memory is forward looking, helping us anticipate the future with knowledge from the past. Prospective memory aligns with hope as a pathway for our thoughts about the future. Hope has importance for human survival, motivating us to set goals, invest in change, and cope. The mental time travel of hope can structure our lives, influence our present state of mind, and alter our behaviors. Whereas hopelessness is associated with depression and anxiety, hope means we can learn from the challenges we encounter in life, responding to emotions by projecting what we learn onto an anticipated future.

Reflections

- In what ways have you experienced feeling lost in response to loss?
- What have you learned from a deceased loved one, namely, how has your memory of them provided information in your present life and affected your future plans?
- Having hope means we can learn from challenges that we encounter in life, be guided by our memories of a deceased loved one and by those who are living, and project what we learn onto an anticipated future that has meaning for us. Describe the hopes you hold in your life since your loss.

USEFUL DEFINITIONS

Affect: The biological source of emotion and feeling, which may be positive, negative, or neutral.

Ambivalent affect: The simultaneous experience of emotion as both positive and negative.

Autobiographical memory: The recollection of a sequence of personally significant experiences that provides knowledge of the self in the past that allows us to project our self into the future.

Basic emotion: see Primary emotion.

Broken heart syndrome: A temporary and reversible condition that is triggered by sudden emotional or physical stress. Also known as "takotsubo cardiomyopathy" or stress "cardiomyopathy."

Competing memories: The interference between memories or a distortion of a memory based on the enormous amount of information we hold about the past.

Complicated grief: A persistent and heightened state of mourning involving specific symptoms. In other contexts, similar designations are "prolonged grief disorder" or "persistent complex bereavement disorder."

Constructive memory: A memory process that pieces together fragments of stored information that are influenced by current knowledge, attitudes, and beliefs.

Core emotion: see Primary emotion.

Ecphory (ecphoric sensation): Memories that are activated by a situation, event, person, or circumstance in the present that matches the information stored in memory.

Emotional memory: Memories related to emotional events or to stimuli that occurred in an emotional context, or a consciously remembered experience that activates an emotional reaction.

Emotional state: The subjective experience of emotion, including physiological arousal and the appraisal of what we feel on the basis of our prior experiences, culture, and the environment in which we were raised.

Episodic memory: Intentionally or consciously recalled memories of sensations, emotions, and associations related to significant personal experiences.

Explicit memory: Consciously recalled factual and autobiographical information.

Flashbulb memory: Vivid but brief perceptual memory fragment (visual image) or isolated details of a scene experienced during an event.

Imagery: Mental or imaginary images representing our thoughts and feelings.

Implicit memory: A memory that occurs without conscious processing or recognition of how past experiences influence present reality.

Involuntary memory: A memory that occurs without our conscious effort when certain cues encountered in everyday life trigger recollections of the past. Also known as "involuntary explicit memory," "involuntary autobiographical memory," "involuntary conscious memory," and "the Proust phenomenon."

Narrative self or narrative self-definition: The accumulated autobiographical memories and future intentions (a self with a past and future) that represent our self-image, including autobiographical memories based on experiences of grief.

Persistent complex bereavement disorder: A persistent and heightened state of mourning characterized by specific symptoms. The designation is included in the fifth edition of the American Psychiatric Association's (2013) *Diagnostic and Statistical Manual of Mental Disorders* under the category "Other Specified Trauma and Stressor Related Disorder." Also referred to as "prolonged grief disorder."

Primal scene: In psychoanalytic theory, the primal scene connotes a traumatic experience of a child's observation or unconscious fantasy of a sexual act between the parents.

Primary emotion: A classification of emotions that are universally recognized and expressed across cultures.

Prolonged grief disorder: A persistent and heightened state of mourning with specific symptoms lasting at least 6 months after a loss, as described in the World Health Organization's (2022) *International Statistical Classification of Diseases and Related Health Problems*. In other contexts, it is referred to as "persistent complex bereavement disorder."

Prospective memory: Memory involving time, event, and activity; the recall of what we intend to do at a future point.

Rapid eye movement (REM) sleep: A phase of sleep characterized by desynchronized brain waves, rapid movement of the eyes, low muscle tone, and vivid dreaming, which may help the consolidation of certain forms of memories.

Self-defining memory: As an aspect of autobiographical memory, self-defining memory involves scenes of a remembered self or life-story reference points that carry an emotional charge.

Semantic memory: The recollection of general knowledge, such as facts or concepts.

REFERENCES

Abramson, L. Y., Metalsky, G. I., & Alloy, L. B. (1989). Hopelessness depression: A theory-based subtype of depression. *Psychological Review*, 96(2), 358–372. https://doi.org/10.1037/0033-295X.96.2.358

Acevedo, B. P., & Aron, A. (2009). Does a long-term relationship kill romantic love? *Review of General Psychology*, 13(1), 59–65. https://doi.org/10.1037/a0014226

Addis, D. R., Wong, A. T., & Schacter, D. L. (2008). Age-related changes in the episodic simulation of future events. *Psychological Science*, 19(1), 33–41. https://doi.org/10.1111/j.1467-9280.2008.02043.x

American Psychiatric Association. (2013). *Diagnostic and statistical manual of mental disorders* (5th ed.). https://doi.org/10.1176/appi.books.9780890425596

Anderson, M. C., & Levy, B. J. (2009). Suppressing unwanted memories. *Current Directions in Psychological Science*, 18(4), 189–194. https://doi.org/10.1111/j.1467-8721.2009.01634.x

Anderson, M. S. F. (2020). *A qualitative exploration of the continued sibling relationship following the sudden death of a sibling in adulthood* [Unpublished doctoral dissertation]. The Wright Institute.

Archer, J. (1999). *The nature of grief: The evolution and psychology of reactions to loss*. Routledge. https://doi.org/10.4324/9780203360651

Aron, A., Paris, M., & Aron, E. N. (1995). Falling in love: Prospective studies of self-concept change. *Journal of Personality and Social Psychology*, 69(6), 1102–1112. https://doi.org/10.1037/0022-3514.69.6.1102

Aston-Jones, G., & Cohen, J. D. (2005). An integrative theory of locus coeruleus–norepinephrine function: Adaptive gain and optimal performance. *Annual Review of Neuroscience, 28*, 403–450. https://doi.org/10.1146/annurev.neuro.28.061604.135709

Avis, N. E., Brambilla, D. J., Vass, K., & McKinlay, J. B. (1991). The effect of widowhood on health: A prospective analysis from the Massachusetts Women's Health Study. *Social Science & Medicine, 33*(9), 1063–1070. https://doi.org/10.1016/0277-9536(91)90011-Z

Baddeley, A. (1988). But what the hell is it for? In M. M. Gruneberg, P. E. Morris, & R. N. Sykes (Eds.), *Practical aspects of memory: Current research and issues, Vol. 1. Memory in everyday life* (pp. 3–18). Wiley.

Baddeley, J., & Singer, J. A. (2010). A loss in the family: Silence, memory, and narrative identity after bereavement. *Memory, 18*(2), 198–207. https://doi.org/10.1080/09658210903143858

Badia, M. (2019). *Grief and the search for meaning: The role of merged identity and identity disruption* [Unpublished doctoral dissertation]. Pace University. https://digitalcommons.pace.edu/dissertations/AAI22589760

Balint, M. (1969). *The basic fault: Therapeutic aspects of regression.* Brunner/Mazel.

Basten, C., & Touyz, S. (2020). Sense of self: Its place in personality disturbance, psychopathology, and normal experience. *Review of General Psychology, 24*(2), 159–171. https://doi.org/10.1177/1089268019880884

Beck, A. T. (1964). Thinking and depression: II. Theory and therapy. *Achieves of General Psychiatry, 10*(6), 561–571. https://doi.org/10.1001/archpsyc.1964.01720240015003

Beck, A. T. (1972). *Depression: Causes and treatment.* University of Pennsylvania Press.

Beck, J. S. (2011). *Cognitive behavioral therapy: Basics and beyond* (2nd ed.). Guilford Press.

Bellet, B. W., Jones, P. J., Meyersburg, C. A., Brenneman, M. M., Morehead, K. E., & McNally, R. J. (2020). Trigger warnings and resilience in college students: A preregistered replication and extension. *Journal of Experimental Psychology: Applied, 26*(4), 717–723. https://doi.org/10.1037/xap0000270

Bellet, B. W., LeBlanc, N. J., Nizzi, M.-C., Carter, M. L., van der Does, F. H. S., Peters, J., Robinaugh, D. J., & McNally, R. J. (2020). Identity confusion in complicated grief: A closer look. *Journal of Abnormal Psychology, 129*(4), 397–407. https://doi.org/10.1037/abn0000520

Berman, E. (2001). Psychoanalysis and life. *The Psychoanalytic Quarterly, 70*(1), 35–65. https://doi.org/10.1002/j.2167-4086.2001.tb00589.x

Berntsen, D., & Rubin, D. C. (2006). The Centrality of Event Scale: A measure of integrating a trauma into one's identity and its relation to post-traumatic stress disorder symptoms. *Behaviour Research and Therapy, 44*(2), 219–231. https://doi.org/10.1016/j.brat.2005.01.009

Beversdorf, D. Q., Hughes, J. D., Steinberg, B. A., Lewis, L. D., & Heilman, K. M. (1999). Noradrenergic modulation of cognitive flexibility in problem solving. *NeuroReport, 10*(13), 2763–2767. https://doi.org/10.1097/00001756-199909090-00012

Black, J., Belicki, K., Piro, R., & Hughes, H. (2021). Comforting versus distressing dreams of the deceased: Relations to grief, trauma, attachment, continuing bonds, and post-dream reactions. *Omega, 84*(2), 525–550. https://doi.org/10.1177/0030222820903850

Bloom, R. (Composer), & Gallop, S. (Lyricist). (1947). *Maybe you'll be there* [Song]. Triangle Music Corporation. https://digitalcommons.library.umaine.edu/mmb-vp-copyright/1805

Bluck, S. (2003). Autobiographical memory: Exploring its functions in everyday life. *Memory, 11*(2), 113–123. https://doi.org/10.1080/741938206

Bluck, S., & Li, K. Z. H. (2001). Predicting memory completeness and accuracy: Emotion and exposure in repeated autobiographical recall. *Applied Cognitive Psychology, 15*(2), 145–158. https://doi.org/10.1002/1099-0720(200103/04)15:2<145::AID-ACP693>3.0.CO;2-T

Blunt, E. (2018). *The place where the lost things go* [Song]. https://www.songfacts.com/lyrics/emily-blunt/the-place-where-lost-things-go

Bohm, D. (1987). *Unfolding meaning*. Routledge.

Bonanno, G. A. (2004). Loss, trauma, and human resilience: Have we underestimated the human capacity to thrive after extremely aversive events? *American Psychologist, 59*(1), 20–28. https://doi.org/10.1037/0003-066X.59.1.20

Bonanno, G. A. (2005). Resilience in the face of potential trauma. *Current Directions in Psychological Science, 14*(3), 135–138. https://doi.org/10.1111/j.0963-7214.2005.00347.x

Bonanno, G. A. (2010). *The other side of sadness: What the new science of bereavement tells us about life after loss*. Basic Books.

Bonanno, G. A. (2012). Emotional dissociation, self-deception, and adaptation to loss. In C. R. Figley (Ed.), *Traumatology of grieving: Conceptual, theoretical, and treatment foundations* (pp. 89–108). Routledge.

Bonanno, G. A., & Keltner, D. (1997). Facial expressions of emotion and the course of conjugal bereavement. *Journal of Abnormal Psychology, 106*(1), 126–137. https://doi.org/10.1037/0021-843X.106.1.126

Bonanno, G. A., Moskowitz, J. T., Papa, A., & Folkman, S. (2005). Resilience to loss in bereaved spouses, bereaved parents, and bereaved gay men. *Journal of Personality and Social Psychology, 88*(5), 827–843. https://doi.org/10.1037/0022-3514.88.5.827

Bonanno, G. A., Papa, A., & O'Neill, K. (2001). Loss and human resilience. *Applied & Preventive Psychology, 10*(3), 193–206. https://doi.org/10.1016/S0962-1849(01)80014-7

Bonanno, G. A., Wortman, C. B., Lehman, D. R., Tweed, R. G., Haring, M., Sonnega, J., Carr, D., & Nesse, R. M. (2002). Resilience to loss and chronic grief: A prospective study from preloss to 18-months postloss. *Journal of Personality and Social Psychology, 83*(5), 1150–1164. https://doi.org/10.1037//0022-3514.83.5.1150

Bonanno, G. A., Wortman, C. B., & Nesse, R. M. (2004). Prospective patterns of resilience and maladjustment during widowhood. *Psychology and Aging, 19*(2), 260–271. https://doi.org/10.1037/0882-7974.19.2.260

Bouret, S., & Sara, S. J. (2005). Network reset: A simplified overarching theory of locus coeruleus noradrenaline function. *Trends in Neuroscience, 28*(11), 574–582. https://doi.org/10.1016/j.tins.2005.09.002

Bower, G. H., & Sivers, H. (1998). Cognitive impact of traumatic events. *Development and Psychopathology, 10*(4), 625–653. https://doi.org/10.1017/S0954579498001795

Bowlby, J. (1961). Processes of mourning. *The International Journal of Psycho-Analysis, 42*, 317–340.

Bowlby, J. (1980). *Attachment and loss: Volume III. Loss, sadness, and depression.* Basic Books.

Bowlby, J., & Parkes, C. M. (1970). Separation and loss within the family. In E. J. Anthony & C. Koupernik (Eds.), *The child and his family* (pp. 197–216). Wiley.

Bowlby, J., Robertson, J., & Rosenbluth, D. (1952). A two-year-old goes to hospital. *The Psychoanalytic Study of the Child, 7*(1), 82–94.

Boyer, P. (2008). Evolutionary economics of mental time travel? *Trends in Cognitive Sciences, 12*(6), P219–P224. https://doi.org/10.1016/j.tics. 2008.03.003

Boyraz, G., Horne, S. G., & Waits, J. B. (2015). Accepting death as part of life: Meaning in life as a means for dealing with loss among bereaved individuals. *Death Studies, 39*(1), 1–11. https://doi.org/10.1080/ 07481187.2013.878767

Brewin, C. R. (2016). Coherence, disorganization, and fragmentation in traumatic memory reconsidered: A response to Rubin et al. (2016). *Journal of Abnormal Psychology, 125*(7), 1011–1017. https://doi.org/ 10.1037/abn0000154

Brewin, C. R., Andrews, B., & Mickes, L. (2020). Regaining consensus on the reliability of memory. *Current Directions in Psychological Science, 29*(2), 121–125. https://doi.org/10.1177/0963721419898122

Brewin, C. R., Gregory, J. D., Lipton, M., & Burgess, N. (2010). Intrusive images in psychological disorders: Characteristics, neural mechanisms, and treatment implications. *Psychological Review, 117*(1), 210–232. https://doi.org/10.1037/a0018113

Broadbridge, C. L. (2018). Is the centralization of potentially traumatic events always negative? An expansion of the Centrality of Events Scale. *Applied Cognitive Psychology, 32*(3), 315–325. https://doi.org/ 10.1002/acp.3403

Brod, G., Werkle-Bergner, M., & Shing, Y. L. (2013). The influence of prior knowledge on memory: A developmental cognitive neuroscience perspective. *Frontiers in Behavioral Neuroscience, 7*, 139. https://doi.org/ 10.3389/fnbeh.2013.00139

Bromberg, P. (2009). Truth, human relatedness, and the analytic process: An interpersonal/relational perspective. *International Journal of Psychoanalysis, 90*(2), 347–361. https://doi.org/10.1111/j.1745-8315. 2009.00137.x

Brown, R., & Kulik, J. (1977). Flashbulb memories. *Cognition, 5*(1), 73–99. https://doi.org/10.1016/0010-0277(77)90018-X

Bruininks, P., & Malle, B. F. (2005). Distinguishing hope from optimism and related affective states. *Motivation and Emotion, 29*(4), 324–352. https://doi.org/10.1007/s11031-006-9010-4

Brumley, A. E. (Composer). (1932). *I'll fly away*. Albert E. Brumley and Sons.

Buchanan, T. W., & Adolphs, R. (2004). The neuroanatomy of emotional memory in humans. In D. Reisberg & P. Hertel (Eds.), *Memory and emotion* (pp. 42–75). Oxford University Press. https://doi.org/10.1093/acprof:oso/9780195158564.003.0002

Buckley, T., Sunari, D., Marshall, A., Bartrop, R., McKinley, S., & Tofler, G. (2012). Physiological correlates of bereavement and the impact of bereavement interventions. *Dialogues in Clinical Neuroscience, 14*(2), 129–139. https://doi.org/10.31887/DCNS.2012.14.2/tbuckley

Butler, E. A., & Randall, A. K. (2013). Emotional coregulation in close relationships. *Emotion Review, 5*(2), 202–210. https://doi.org/10.1177/1754073912451630

Butner, J., Diamond, L. M., & Hicks, A. M. (2007). Attachment style and two forms of affect coregulation between romantic partners. *Personal Relationships, 14*(3), 431–455. https://doi.org/10.1111/j.1475-6811.2007.00164.x

Cabeza, R., & St. Jacques, P. (2007). Functional neuroimaging of autobiographical memory. *Trends in Cognitive Sciences, 11*(5), P219–P227. https://doi.org/10.1016/j.tics.2007.02.005

Carr, D., House, J. S., Kessler, R. C., Nesse, R. M., Sonnega, J., & Wortman, C. (2000). Marital quality and psychological adjustment to widowhood among older adults: A longitudinal analysis. *The Journals of Gerontology: Series B. Psychological Sciences and Social Sciences, 55*(4), S197–S207. https://doi.org/10.1093/geronb/55.4.S197

Clark, D. M., & Wells, A. (1995). A cognitive model of social phobia. In R. G. Heimberg, M. R. Liebowitz, D. A. Hope, & F. R. Schneier (Eds.), *Social phobia: Diagnosis, assessment, and treatment* (pp. 69–93). Guilford Press.

Clewell, T. (2004). Mourning beyond melancholia: Freud's psychoanalysis of loss. *Journal of the American Psychoanalytic Association, 52*(1), 43–67. https://doi.org/10.1177/00030651040520010601

Conway, M. A., & Pleydell-Pearce, C. W. (2000). The construction of autobiographical memories in the self-memory system. *Psychological Review, 107*(2), 261–288. https://doi.org/10.1037/0033-295x.107.2.261

Craik, F. I. M., & Tulving, E. (1975). Depth of processing and the retention of words in episodic memory. *Journal of Experimental Psychology:*

General, 104(3), 268–294. https://doi.org/10.1037/0096-3445.104.3.268

Czub, T. (2013). Shame as a self-conscious emotion and its role in identity formation. *Polish Psychological Bulletin, 44*(3), 245–253. https://doi.org/10.2478/ppb-2013-0028

Daleiden, E. L., & Vasey, M. W. (1997). An information-processing perspective on childhood anxiety. *Clinical Psychology Review, 17*(4), 407–429. https://doi.org/10.1016/s0272-7358(97)00010-x

Daly, L. M. (2020). Resilience: An integrated review. *Nursing Science Quarterly, 33*(4), 330–338. https://doi.org/10.1177/0894318420943141

Damasio, A. (2000). *The feeling of what happens: Body, emotion and the making of consciousness.* Mariner Books.

Datson, S. L., & Marwit, S. J. (1997). Personality constructs and perceived presence of deceased loved ones. *Death Studies, 21*(2), 131–146. https://doi.org/10.1080/074811897202047

Davidai, S., & Gilovich, T. (2018). The ideal road not taken: The self-discrepancies involved in people's most enduring regrets. *Emotion, 18*(3), 439–452. https://doi.org/10.1037/emo0000326

Davis, C. G., Lehman, D. R., Wortman, C. B., Silver, R. C., & Thompson, S. C. (1995). The undoing of traumatic life events. *Personality and Social Psychology Bulletin, 21*(2), 109–124. https://doi.org/10.1177/0146167295212002

Davis, C. G., Nolen-Hoeksema, S., & Larson, J. (1998). Making sense of loss and benefiting from the experience: Two construals of meaning. *Journal of Personality and Social Psychology, 75*(2), 561–574. https://doi.org/10.1037/0022-3514.75.2.561

Davis, M. C., Zautra, A. J., & Smith, B. W. (2004). Chronic pain, stress, and the dynamics of affective differentiation. *Journal of Personality, 72*(6), 1133–1160. https://doi.org/10.1111/j.1467-6494.2004.00293.x

Dellmann, T. (2018). Are shame and self-esteem risk factors in prolonged grief after death of a spouse? *Death Studies, 42*(6), 371–382. https://doi.org/10.1080/07481187.2017.1351501

Demos, E. V. (2001). Psychoanalysis and the human sciences: The limitations of cut-and-paste theorizing. *American Imago, 58*(3), 649–684. https://doi.org/10.1353/aim.2001.0012

Denckla, C. A., Mancini, A. D., Bornstein, R. F., & Bonanno, G. A. (2011). Adaptive and maladaptive dependency in bereavement: Distinguishing prolonged and resolved grief trajectories. *Personality and Individual Differences, 51*(8), 1012–1017. https://doi.org/10.1016/j.paid.2011.08.014

Dennett, D. (1992). The self as the center of narrative gravity. In F. S. Kessel, P. M. Cole, & D. L. Johnson (Eds.), *Self and consciousness: Multiple perspectives* (pp. 103–115). Erlbaum.

Depue, B. E., Curran, T., & Banich, M. T. (2007, July 13). Prefrontal regions orchestrate suppression of emotional memories via a two-phase process. *Science, 317*(5835), 215–219. https://doi.org/10.1126/science.1139560

Diamond, N. B., Armson, M. J., & Levine, B. (2020). The truth is out there: Accuracy in recall of verifiable real-world events. *Psychological Science, 31*(12), 1544–1556. https://doi.org/10.1177/0956797620954812

Diamond, N. B., & Levine, B. (2020). Linking detail to temporal structure in naturalistic-event recall. *Psychological Science, 31*(12), 1557–1572. https://doi.org/10.1177/0956797620958651

Doka, K. J. (1989). *Disenfranchised grief: Recognizing hidden sorrow.* Lexington Books.

Ehlers, A., & Clark, D. M. (2000). A cognitive model of posttraumatic stress disorder. *Behaviour Research and Therapy, 38*(4), 319–345. https://doi.org/10.1016/s0005-7967(99)00123-0

Ehlers, A., Hackmann, A., & Michael, T. (2004). Intrusive re-experiencing in post-traumatic stress disorder: Phenomenology, theory, and therapy. *Memory, 12*(4), 403–415. https://doi.org/10.1080/09658210444000025

Ekman, P. (2003). *Emotions revealed: Recognizing faces and feelings to improve communication and emotional life.* Henry Holt.

Elison, J., & McGonigle, C. (2003). *Liberating losses: When death brings relief.* Perseus.

Eplett, L. (2012, August 8). Fava—The magic bean [Guest blog]. *Scientific American.* https://blogs.scientificamerican.com/guest-blog/fava-the-magic-bean/

Feder, A., Schmajuk, M., Charney, D. S., & Southwick, S. M. (2016). Resilience. In A. B. Simon, A. S. New, & W. K. Goodman (Eds.), *Mount Sinai expert guides: Psychiatry* (pp. 356–361). Wiley-Blackwell. https://doi.org/10.1002/9781118654231.ch41

Feldman Barrett, L., Gross, J., Christensen, T. C., & Benvenuto, M. (2001). Knowing what you're feeling and knowing what to do about it: Mapping the relation between emotion differentiation and emotion regulation. *Cognition and Emotion, 15*(6), 713–724. https://doi.org/ 10.1080/02699930143000239

Field, N. P., & Sundin, E. C. (2001). Attachment style in adjustment to conjugal bereavement. *Journal of Social and Personal Relationships, 18*(3), 347–361. https://doi.org/10.1177/0265407501183003

Field, T. (2009). *Complementary and alternative therapies research.* American Psychological Association. https://doi.org/10.1037/11859-000

Field, T. (2012). Relationships as regulators. *Psychology, 3*(6), 467–479. https://doi.org/10.4236/psych.2012.36066

Field, T., Diego, M., & Hernandez-Reif, M. (2007). Massage therapy research. *Developmental Review, 27*(1), 75–89. https://doi.org/10.1016/ j.dr.2005.12.002

FitzGibbon, L., Komiya, A., & Murayama, K. (2021). The lure of counterfactual curiosity: People incur a cost to experience regret. *Psychological Science, 32*(2), 241–255. https://doi.org/10.1177/0956797620963615

Fivush, R. (2018). The sociocultural functions of episodic memory. *Behavioral and Brain Sciences, 41*, E14. https://doi.org/10.1017/ S0140525X17001352

Fogel, A., & Garvey, A. (2007). Alive communication. *Infant Behavior & Development, 30*(2), 251–257. https://doi.org/10.1016/j.infbeh.2007.02.007

Fraley, R. C., & Bonanno, G. A. (2004). Attachment and loss: A test of three competing models on the association between attachment-related avoidance and adaptation to bereavement. *Personality and Social Psychology Bulletin, 30*(7), 878–890. https://doi.org/10.1177/0146167204264289

Freed, P. J., Yanagihara, T. K., Hirsch, J., & Mann, J. J. (2009). Neural mechanisms of grief regulation. *Biological Psychiatry, 66*(1), 33–40. https:// doi.org/10.1016/j.biopsych.2009.01.019

Freud, S. (1917). Mourning and melancholia. In J. Strachey (Ed. & Trans.), *The standard edition of the complete psychological works of Sigmund Freud: Volume XIV (1914–1916). On the history of the psycho-analytic movement, Papers on metapsychology and other works* (pp. 237–258). Hogarth.

Freud, S. (2000a). Letter from Sigmund Freud to Ernest Jones, March 11, 1928. In P. T. Hoffer (Trans.), *The complete correspondence of Sigmund Freud and Ernest Jones 1908–1939* (pp. 643–644). Belknap Press.

Freud, S. (2000b). Letter from Sigmund Freud to Sándor Ferenczi, January 29, 1920. In P. T. Hoffer (Trans.), *The correspondence of Sigmund Freud and Sándor Ferenczi: Vol. 3. 1920–1933* (p. 6). Belknap Press.

Freud, S. (2003). Letter from Sigmund Freud to Ludwig Binswanger, November 29, 1926. In G. Fichtner & L. Binswanger (Eds.), *The Sigmund Freud–Ludwig Binswanger correspondence 1908–1938* (pp. 185–186). Other Press.

Friedman, L. J. (1999). *Identity's architect: A biography of Erik H. Erikson.* Scribner.

Frost, L., & Hoggett, P. (2008). Human agency and social suffering. *Critical Social Policy, 28*(4), 438–460. https://doi.org/10.1177/0261018308095279

Fuchs, T. (2018). Presence in absence: The ambiguous phenomenology of grief. *Phenomenology and the Cognitive Sciences, 17*(1), 43–63. https://doi.org/10.1007/s11097-017-9506-2

Gable, S. L., & Haidt, J. (2005). What (and why) is positive psychology? *Review of General Psychology, 9*(2), 103–110. https://doi.org/10.1037/1089-2680.9.2.103

Gagnepain, P., Hulbert, J., & Anderson, M. C. (2017). Parallel regulation of memory and emotion supports the suppression of intrusive memories. *Journal of Neuroscience, 37*(27), 6423–6441. https://doi.org/10.1523/JNEUROSCI.2732-16.2017

Gallagher, S. (2000). Philosophical conceptions of the self: Implications for cognitive science. *Trends in Cognitive Sciences, 4*(1), 14–21. https://doi.org/10.1016/s1364-6613(99)01417-5

Gallo, D. A., & Wheeler, M. E. (2013). Episodic memory. In D. Reisberg (Ed.), *The Oxford handbook of cognitive psychology* (pp. 189–205). Oxford University Press.

Gardner, R. S., & Ascoli, G. A. (2015). The natural frequency of human prospective memory increases with age. *Psychology and Aging, 30*(2), 209–219. https://doi.org/10.1037/a0038876

Gasper, K., Spencer, L. A., & Middlewood, B. L. (2020). Differentiating hope from optimism by examining self-reported appraisals and linguistic content. *The Journal of Positive Psychology, 15*(2), 220–237. https://doi.org/10.1080/17439760.2019.1590623

Germain, A., Caroff, K., Buysse, D. J., & Shear, M. K. (2005). Sleep quality in complicated grief. *Journal of Traumatic Stress, 18*(4), 343–346. https://doi.org/10.1002/jts.20035

Getz, L., & Carter, C. (1996). Prairie-vole partnerships. *American Scientist, 84*(1), 56–62.

Getz, L. L., McGuire, B., Pizzuto, T., Hofmann, J. E., & Frase, B. (1993). Social organization of the prairie vole (*Microtus ochrogaster*). *Journal of Mammalogy*, *74*(1), 44–58.

Gillies, J., & Neimeyer, R. A. (2006). Loss, grief, and the search for significance: Toward a model of meaning reconstruction in bereavement. *Journal of Constructivist Psychology*, *19*(1), 31–65. https://doi.org/10.1080/10720530500311182

Gloede, M. E., Paulauskas, E. E., & Gregg, M. K. (2017). Experience and information loss in auditory and visual memory. *Quarterly Journal of Experimental Psychology*, *70*(7), 1344–1352. https://doi.org/10.1080/17470218.2016.1183686

Guo, J., Klevan, M., & McAdams, D. P. (2016). Personality traits, ego development, and the redemptive self. *Personality and Social Psychology Bulletin*, *42*(11), 1551–1563. https://doi.org/10.1177/0146167216665093

Hackmann, A. (1998). Working with images in clinical psychology. In A. S. Bellack & M. Hersen (Eds.), *Comprehensive clinical psychology* (Vol. 6, pp. 301–318). Elsevier.

Hall, C. (2014). Bereavement theory: Recent developments in our understanding of grief and bereavement. *Bereavement Care*, *33*(1), 7–12. https://doi.org/10.1080/02682621.2014.902610

Harber, K. D., & Pennebaker, J. W. (1992). Overcoming traumatic memories. In S.-Å. Christianson (Ed.), *The handbook of emotion and memory: Research and theory* (pp. 359–387). Erlbaum.

Helgeson, V. S., Reynolds, K. A., & Tomich, P. L. (2006). A meta-analytic review of benefit finding and growth. *Journal of Consulting and Clinical Psychology*, *74*(5), 797–816. https://doi.org/10.1037/0022-006X.74.5.797

Henretty, J. R., Levitt, H. M., & Mathews, S. S. (2008). Clients' experiences of moments of sadness in psychotherapy: A grounded theory analysis. *Psychotherapy Research*, *18*(3), 243–255. https://doi.org/10.1080/10503300701765831

Herz, R. S., Eliassen, J., Beland, S., & Souza, T. (2004). Neuroimaging evidence for the emotional potency of odor-evoked memory. *Neuropsychologia*, *42*(3), 371–378. https://doi.org/10.1016/j.neuropsychologia.2003.08.009

Hofer, M. A. (1984). Relationships as regulators: A psychobiologic perspective on bereavement. *Psychosomatic Medicine, 46*(3), 183–197. https://doi.org/10.1097/00006842-198405000-00001

Hofer, M. K., & Chen, F. S. (2020). The scent of a good night's sleep: Olfactory cues of a romantic partner improve sleep efficiency. *Psychological Science, 31*(4), 449–459. https://doi.org/10.1177/0956797620905615

Hofer, M. K., Chen, F. S., & Schaller, M. (2020). What your nose knows: Affective, cognitive, and behavioral responses to the scent of another person. *Current Directions in Psychological Science, 29*(6), 617–623. https://doi.org/10.1177/0963721420964175

Hofer, M. K., Collins, H. K., Whillans, A. V., & Chen, F. S. (2018). Olfactory cues from romantic partners and strangers influence women's responses to stress. *Journal of Personality and Social Psychology, 114*(1), 1–9. https://doi.org/10.1037/pspa0000110

Holland, J. M., Plant, C. P., Klingspon, K. L., & Neimeyer, R. A. (2020). Bereavement-related regrets and unfinished business with the deceased. *Death Studies, 44*(1), 42–47. https://doi.org/10.1080/07481187.2018.1521106

Holland, J. M., Thompson, K. L., Rozalski, V., & Lichtenthal, W. G. (2014). Bereavement-related regret trajectories among widowed older adults. *Journals of Gerontology: Series B. Psychological Sciences and Social Sciences, 69B*(1), 40–47. https://doi.org/10.1093/geronb/gbt050

Horowitz, M. J. (1976). *Stress response syndromes.* Jason Aronson.

Ingvar, D. H. (1985). "Memory of the future": An essay on the temporal organization of conscious awareness. *Human Neurobiology, 4*(3), 127–136.

Izard, C. (1977). *Human emotions.* Plenum Press.

James, W. (1950). *The principles of psychology.* Dover. (Original work published 1890)

Johnson, H. M., & Seifert, C. M. (1994). Sources of the continued influence effect: When misinformation in memory affects later inferences. *Journal of Experimental Psychology: Learning, Memory, and Cognition, 20*(6), 1420–1436. https://doi.org/10.1037/0278-7393.20.6.1420

Johnson, J. G., Vanderwerker, L. C., Bornstein, R. F., Zhang, B., & Prigerson, H. G. (2006). Development and validation of an instrument for the assessment of dependency among bereaved persons. *Journal of Psychopathology and Behavioral Assessment, 28,* 261–270. https://doi.org/10.1007/s10862-005-9016-3

Kandel, E. R. (1998). A new intellectual framework for psychiatry. *American Journal of Psychiatry, 155*(4), 457–469. https://doi.org/10.1176/ajp.155.4.457

Kauffman, J. (Ed.). (2002a). *Loss of the assumptive world: A theory of traumatic loss.* Brunner-Routledge.

Kauffman, J. (2002b). Safety and the assumptive world: A theory of traumatic loss. In J. Kauffman (Ed.), *Loss of the assumptive world: A theory of traumatic loss* (pp. 205–212). Routledge.

Kaufman, G. (1974). The meaning of shame: Toward a self-affirming identity. *Journal of Counseling Psychology, 21*(6), 568–574. https://doi.org/10.1037/h0037251

Keltner, D., & Bonanno, G. A. (1997). A study of laughter and dissociation: Distinct correlates of laughter and smiling during bereavement. *Journal of Personality and Social Psychology, 73*(4), 687–702. https://doi.org/10.1037/0022-3514.73.4.687

Kensinger, E. A., & Schacter, D. L. (2016). Memory and emotion. In M. Lewis, J. M. Haviland-Jones, & L. F. Barrett (Eds.), *Handbook of emotion* (4th ed., pp. 564–578). Guilford Press.

Klass, D., Silverman, P. R., & Nickman, S. L. (Eds.). (1996). *Continuing bonds: New understandings of grief.* Taylor & Francis.

Klingspon, K. L., Holland, J. M., Neimeyer, R. A., & Lichtenthal, W. G. (2015). Unfinished business in bereavement. *Death Studies, 39*(7), 387–398. https://doi.org/10.1080/07481187.2015.1029143

Köhler, W., & von Restorff, H. (1937). Analyse von vorgängen im spurenfeld: Zur theorieder reproduktion [An analysis of the processes in the trace field: Towards a theory of retrieval]. *Psychologische Forschung, 21,* 56–112.

Konderak, P. (2019). Perspectives on the study of meaning-making. In P. Konderak (Ed.), *Cognitive semiotics: Perspectives on the study of meaning-making* (pp. 5–12). Paper & Tinta.

Kosslyn, S. M. (1994). *Image and brain: The resolution of the imagery debate.* MIT Press.

Kowalski, S. D., & Bondmass, M. D. (2008). Physiological and psychological symptoms of grief in widows. *Research in Nursing & Health, 31*(1), 23–30. https://doi.org/10.1002/nur.20228

Krafft, A. M., Guse, T., & Maree, D. (2020). Distinguishing perceived hope and dispositional optimism: Theoretical foundations and empirical findings beyond future expectancies and cognition. *Journal of Well-Being Assessment*, 4, 217–243. https://doi.org/10.1007/s41543-020-00030-4

Kris, E. (1956). The recovery of childhood memories in psychoanalysis. *The Psychoanalytic Study of the Child*, 11, 54–88.

Kübler-Ross, E. (1969). *On death and dying*. Macmillan.

Kübler-Ross, E., & Kessler, D. (2014). *On grief and grieving: Finding the meaning of grief through the five stages of loss*. Scribner.

Kuhl, B. A., Rissman, J., Chun, M. M., & Wagner, A. D. (2011). Fidelity of neural reactivation reveals competition between memories. *Proceedings of the National Academy of Sciences of the United States of America*, 108(14), 5903–5908. https://doi.org/10.1073/pnas.1016939108

Lamia, M. C. (2006). Making psychology a household word—Just for kids. *Professional Psychology: Research and Practice*, 37(2), 114–118. https://doi.org/10.1037/0735-7028.37.2.114

Lamia, M. (2017). *What motivates getting things done: Procrastination, emotions, and success*. Rowman and Littlefield.

Laney, C. (2013). The source of memory errors. In D. Reisberg (Ed.), *The Oxford handbook of cognitive psychology* (pp. 232–242). Oxford University Press.

Lazarus, R. S. (1991). Progress on a cognitive–motivational–relational theory of emotion. *American Psychologist*, 46(8), 819–834. https://doi.org/10.1037/0003-066X.46.8.819

Lazarus, R. S. (1999). Hope: An emotion and a vital coping resource against despair. *Social Research*, 66, 653–678.

Lerner, J. S., & Keltner, D. (2000). Beyond valence: Toward a model of emotion specific influences on judgment and choice. *Cognition and Emotion*, 14(4), 473–493. https://doi.org/10.1080/026999300402763

Lerner, J. S., & Keltner, D. (2001). Fear, anger, and risk. *Journal of Personality and Social Psychology*, 81(1), 146–159. https://doi.org/10.1037/0022-3514.81.1.146

Leu, J., Wang, J., & Koo, K. (2011). Are positive emotions just as "positive" across cultures? *Emotion*, 11(4), 994–999. https://doi.org/10.1037/a0021332

Lewis, H. B. (1971). *Shame and guilt in neurosis*. International Universities Press.

Lewis, H. B. (1987). Shame and the narcissistic personality. In D. L. Nathanson (Ed.), *The many faces of shame* (pp. 93–132). Guilford Press.

Lewis, T. L., Amini, F., & Lannon, R. (2000). *A general theory of love*. Random House.

Lewis Hall, M. E., & Hill, P. (2019). Meaning-making, suffering, and religion: A worldview conception. *Mental Health, Religion & Culture*, 22(5), 467–479. https://doi.org/10.1080/13674676.2019.1625037

Lieberman, M. D., Eisenberger, N. I., Crockett, M. J., Tom, S. M., Pfeifer, J. H., & Way, B. M. (2007). Putting feelings into words: Affect labeling disrupts amygdala activity in response to affective stimuli. *Psychological Science*, 18(5), 421–428. https://doi.org/10.1111/j.1467-9280.2007.01916.x

Lifton, R. J. (1979). *The broken connection: On death and the continuity of life*. American Psychiatric Press.

Lilienfeld, S. O., Lynn, S. J., Ruscio, J., & Beyerstein, B. L. (2010). *50 great myths of popular psychology*. Wiley-Blackwell.

Lin, Y. Y., Servaty-Seib, H. L., & Peterson, J. (2021). Child sexual abuse survivors' grief experiences after the death of the abuser. *Omega*, 83(4), 777–801. https://doi.org/10.1177/0030222819868107

Loftus, E. F. (2003). Make-believe memories. *American Psychologist*, 58(11), 867–873. https://doi.org/10.1037/0003-066X.58.11.867

Longfellow, H. W. (1878). *Kéramos and other poems*. Houghton, Osgood.

Lyubomirsky, S., Dickerhoof, R., Boehm, J. K., & Sheldon, K. M. (2011). Becoming happier takes both a will and a proper way: An experimental longitudinal intervention to boost well-being. *Emotion*, 11(2), 391–402. https://doi.org/10.1037/a0022575

Maccallum, F., & Bryant, R. A. (2008). Self-defining memories in complicated grief. *Behaviour Research and Therapy*, 46(12), 1311–1315. https://doi.org/10.1016/j.brat.2008.09.003

Maccallum, F., & Bryant, R. A. (2010). Attentional bias in complicated grief. *Journal of Affective Disorders*, 125(1–3), 316–322. https://doi.org/10.1016/j.jad.2010.01.070

Maccallum, F., & Bryant, R. A. (2013). A cognitive attachment model of prolonged grief: Integrating attachments, memory, and identity. *Clinical Psychology Review*, 33(6), 713–727. https://doi.org/10.1016/j.cpr.2013.05.001

Maier, S. F., Peterson, C., & Schwartz, B. (2000). From helplessness to hope: The seminal career of Martin Seligman. In J. Gillham (Ed.), *The science of optimism and hope: Research essays in honor of Martin E. Seligman* (pp. 11–37). Templeton Foundation Press.

Marčetić, A. (2017, September 11–16). *The essence of time, a piece of eternity, and Proust's philosophy of identity* [Paper]. Theatrum Mundi VIII, Inter-University Center, Dubrovnik, Croatia.

Marshall, L. S. (2016). Broken heart syndrome. *Journal of Radiology Nursing, 35*(2), 133–137. https://doi.org/10.1016/j.jradnu.2016.04.002

Mashek, D. J., Aron, A., & Boncimino, M. (2003). Confusions of self with close others. *Personality and Social Psychology Bulletin, 29*(3), 382–392. https://doi.org/10.1177/0146167202250220

Mauss, I. B., Savino, N. S., Anderson, C. L., Weisbuch, M., Tamir, M., & Laudenslager, M. L. (2012). The pursuit of happiness can be lonely. *Emotion, 12*(5), 908–912. https://doi.org/10.1037/a0025299

Mayo Clinic Staff. (2020, May 29). *Broken heart syndrome.* https://www.mayoclinic.org/diseases-conditions/broken-heart-syndrome/symptoms-causes/syc-20354617

McAdams, D. P. (1987). A life-story model of identity. In R. Hogan & W. H. Jones (Eds.), *Perspectives in personality* (Vol. 2, pp. 15–50). JAI Press.

McAdams, D. P., & McLean, K. C. (2013). Narrative identity. *Current Directions in Psychological Science, 22*(3), 233–238. https://doi.org/10.1177/0963721413475622

McBride, D. M., & Cutting, J. C. (2016). *Cognitive psychology: Theory, process, and methodology.* Sage.

McBurney, D. H., Shoup, M. L., & Streeter, S. A. (2006). Olfactory comfort: Smelling a partner's clothing during periods of separation. *Journal of Applied Social Psychology, 36*(9), 2325–2335. https://doi.org/10.1111/j.0021-9029.2006.00105.x

McClelland, J. L., McNaughton, B. L., & O'Reilly, R. C. (1995). Why there are complementary learning systems in the hippocampus and neocortex: Insights from the successes and failures of connectionist models of learning and memory. *Psychological Review, 102*(3), 419–457. https://doi.org/10.1037/0033-295X.102.3.419

McClintock, M. K. (1971, January 22). Menstrual synchrony and suppression. *Nature, 229*, 244–245.

McLean, K., Delker, B., Dunlop, W., Salton, R., & Syed, M. (2020). Redemptive stories and those who tell them are preferred in the U.S. *Collabra: Psychology, 6*(1), 39. https://doi.org/10.1525/collabra.369

McLean, K. C., & Syed, M. (2015). Personal, master, and alternative narratives: An integrative framework for understanding identity development in context. *Human Development*, *58*(6), 318–349. https://doi.org/10.1159/000445817

McNally, R. J. (2003). *Remembering trauma*. Belknap Press.

McWilliams, N. (1999). *Psychoanalytic case formulation*. Guilford Press.

Michael, S. T., & Snyder, C. R. (2005). Getting unstuck: The roles of hope, finding meaning, and rumination in the adjustment to bereavement among college students. *Death Studies*, *29*(5), 435–458. https://doi.org/10.1080/07481180590932544

Miranda, M. I. (2012). Taste and odor recognition memory: The emotional flavor of life. *Reviews in the Neurosciences*, *23*(5–6), 481–499. https://doi.org/10.1515/revneuro-2012-0064

Monahan, K. (2003). Death of an abuser: Does the memory linger on? *Death Studies*, *27*(7), 641–651. https://doi.org/10.1080/07481180302899

Morewedge, C. K., Preston, J., & Wegner, D. M. (2007). Timescale bias in the attribution of mind. *Journal of Personality and Social Psychology*, *93*(1), 111. https://doi.org/10.1037/0022-3514.93.1.1

Morrison, A. (1987). The eye turned inward: Shame and the self. In D. L. Nathanson (Ed.), *The many faces of shame* (pp. 271–291). Guilford Press.

Muzzulini, B., Tinti, C., Conway, M., Testa, S., & Schmidt, S. (2020). Flashbulb memory: Referring back to Brown and Kulik's definition. *Memory*, *28*(6), 766–782. https://doi.org/10.1080/09658211.2020.1778035

Nathanson, D. L. (1992). *Shame and pride: Affect, sex, and the birth of the self*. W. W. Norton.

Nebenzahl, I., & Albeck, Y. (1990). The storage and recall of auditory memory. *Journal of Mathematical Biology*, *28*(1), 113–119. https://doi.org/10.1007/BF00171522

Neimeyer, R. A. (2001). Re-authoring life narratives: Grief therapy as meaning reconstruction. *Israel Journal of Psychiatry and Related Sciences*, *38*(3–4), 171–183.

Neimeyer, R. A., Baldwin, S. A., & Gillies, J. (2006). Continuing bonds and reconstructing meaning: Mitigating complications in bereavement. *Death Studies*, *30*(8), 715–738. https://doi.org/10.1080/07481180600848322

Neimeyer, R. A., & Sands, D. C. (2011). Meaning reconstruction in bereavement: From principles to practice. In R. A. Neimeyer, D. L. Harris, H. R. Winokuer, & G. F. Thornton (Eds.), *Grief and bereavement in contemporary society: Bridging research and practice* (pp. 9–22). Routledge.

Neimeyer, R. A., & Thompson, B. E. (2014). *Meaning making and the art of grief therapy*. In B. E. Thompson & R. A. Neimeyer (Eds.), *Grief and the expressive arts: Practices for creating meaning* (pp. 3–13). Routledge.

Neisser, U., & Harsch, N. (1992). Phantom flashbulbs: False recollections of hearing the news about *Challenger*. In E. Winograd & U. Neisser (Eds.), *Affect and accuracy in recall: Studies of flashbulb memories* (pp. 9–31). Cambridge University Press.

Nesse, R. M. (1999). The evolution of hope and despair. *Social Research, 66*(2), 429–469.

Ni, P. (2016). *Visitation dreams of deceased loved ones: Understanding their message, meaning, and transformative power*. Preston Ni Communication Coaching.

Nichols, B. (1951). *Merry Hall*. Jonathan Cape.

O'Connor, M., & McConnell, M. H. (2018). Grief reactions: A neurobiological approach. In E. Bui (Ed.), *Clinical handbook of bereavement and grief reactions* (pp. 45–62). Humana Press.

O'Neil, T. (2020). *Survivors of suicide: Adaptation to traumatic loss and suicide bereavement identity* [Unpublished doctoral dissertation]. The Wright Institute.

Parker, J. S. (2005). Extraordinary experiences of the bereaved and adaptive outcomes of grief. *Omega, 51*, 257–283. https://doi.org/10.2190/FM7M-314B-U3RT-E2CB

Parkes, C. M. (1970). The first year of bereavement: A longitudinal study of the reaction of London widows to the death of their husbands. *Psychiatry, 33*, 444–467.

Parkes, C. M. (2015). *The price of love: The selected works of Colin Murray Parkes*. Routledge.

Parkes, C. M., & Weiss, R. S. (1983). *Recovery from bereavement*. Basic Books.

Pasupathi, M. (2003). Emotion regulation during social remembering: Differences between emotions elicited during an event and emotions elicited when talking about it. *Memory, 11*, 151–163. https://doi.org/10.1080/741938212

Peace, K. A., & Porter, S. (2004). A longitudinal investigation of the reliability of memories for trauma and other emotional experiences. *Applied*

Cognitive Psychology, 18(9), 1143–1159. https://doi.org/10.1002/acp.1046

Pennebaker, J. W., & Seagal, J. D. (1999). Forming a story: The health benefits of narrative. *Journal of Clinical Psychology, 55*, 1243–1254. https://doi.org/10.1002/(SICI)1097-4679(199910)55:10<1243::AID-JCLP6>3.0.CO;2-N

Perry, N. (2000). *Devotion to St. Anthony of Padua* [Blog post]. https://www.franciscanmedia.org/franciscan-spirit-blog/devotion-to-st-anthony-of-padua

Peterson, C., & Park, N. (2003). Positive psychology as the evenhanded positive psychologist views it. *Psychological Inquiry, 14*(2), 143–147.

Peterson, C., & Seligman, M. E. P. (2004). *Character strengths and virtues: A handbook and classification.* American Psychological Association and Oxford University Press.

Phelps, E. A. (2004). Human emotion and memory: Interactions of the amygdala and hippocampal complex. *Current Opinion in Neurobiology, 14*(2), 198–202. https://doi.org/10.1016/j.conb.2004.03.015

Plutchik, R. (2000). *Emotions in the practice of psychotherapy: Clinical implications of affect theories.* American Psychological Association.

Plutchik, R. (2013). *Emotion theory, research, and experience: Volume 5. Emotion, psychopathology, and psychotherapy.* Academic Press.

Prebble, S. C., Addis, D. R., & Tippett, L. J. (2013). Autobiographical memory and sense of self. *Psychological Bulletin, 139*(4), 815–840. https://doi.org/10.1037/a0030146

Prigerson, H. G., Wolfson, L., Shear, M. K., Hall, M., Bierhals, A. J., Zonarich, D. L., Pilkonis, P. A., & Reynolds, C. F., III. (1997). Case histories of traumatic grief. *Omega, 35*, 9–24. https://doi.org/10.2190/TDYG-MRB4-H5H8-HHR7

Proust, M. (1928). Remembrance of things past: Vol. 1. Swann's Way: Within a budding grove. In C. K. S. Moncrieff & T. Kilmartin (Trans.), *The definitive French pleiade* (pp. 48–51). Vintage Books.

Read, R. (2018). Can there be a logic of grief? Why Wittgenstein and Merleau-Ponty say "yes." In O. Kuusela, M. Ometita, & T. Ucan (Eds.), *Wittgenstein and phenomenology* (pp. 176–196). Routledge.

Rees, D. (2001). *Death and bereavement: The psychological, religious and cultural interfaces.* Wiley.

Richardson, V. E., Bennett, K. M., Carr, D., Gallagher, S., Kim, J., & Fields, N. (2015). How does bereavement get under the skin? The effects of late-life spousal loss on cortisol levels. *Journals of Gerontology: Series B. Psychological Sciences and Social Sciences*, 70(3), 341–347. https://doi.org/10.1093/geronb/gbt116

Richmond, J., & Nelson, C. A. (2007). Accounting for change in declarative memory: A cognitive neuroscience perspective. *Developmental Review*, 27(3), 349–373. https://doi.org/10.1016/j.dr.2007.04.002

Rilke, R. M. (1995). Love song. In S. Mitchell (Trans.), *Ahead of all parting: The selected poetry and prose of Rainer Maria Rilke* (pp. 29–30). Random House. (Original work published 1907)

Robinaugh, D. J., & McNally, R. J. (2013). Remembering the past and envisioning the future in bereaved adults with and without complicated grief. *Clinical Psychological Science*, 1(3), 290–300. https://doi.org/10.1177/2167702613476027

Robinson, J. (1986). Autobiographical memory: A historical prologue. In D. Rubin (Ed.), *Auto-biographical memory* (pp. 19–24). Cambridge University Press.

Roese, N. J., & Summerville, A. (2005). Why we regret most . . . and why. *Personality and Social Psychology Bulletin*, 31(9), 1273–1285. https://doi.org/10.1177/0146167205274693

Ross, M., & Wilson, A. E. (2003). Autobiographical memory and conceptions of self: Getting better all the time. *Current Directions in Psychological Science*, 12(2), 66–69. https://doi.org/10.1111/1467-8721.01228

Rothbaum, F., & Tsang, B. Y. P. (1998). Lovesongs in the United States and China: On the nature of romantic love. *Journal of Cross-Cultural Psychology*, 29(2), 306–319. https://doi.org/10.1177/0022022198292003

Rubin, D. C., Boals, A., & Berntsen, D. (2008). Memory in posttraumatic stress disorder: Properties of voluntary and involuntary, traumatic and nontraumatic autobiographical memories in people with and without posttraumatic stress disorder symptoms. *Journal of Experimental Psychology: General*, 137(4), 591–614. https://doi.org/10.1037/a0013165

Salovey, P., Bedell, B. T., Detweiler, J. B., & Mayer, J. D. (1999). Coping intelligently: Emotional intelligence and the coping process. In C. R. Snyder (Ed.), *Coping: The psychology of what works* (pp. 141–164). Oxford University Press.

Saudade. (2021, August 15). In *Wikipedia*. https://en.wikipedia.org/wiki/Saudade

Sbarra, D. A., & Hazan, C. (2008). Coregulation, dysregulation, self-regulation: An integrative analysis and empirical agenda for understanding adult attachment, separation, loss, and recovery. *Personality and Social Psychology Review*, *12*(2), 141–167. https://doi.org/10.1177/1088868308315702

Scarpelli, S., Bartolacci, C., D'Atri, A., Gorgoni, M., & De Gennaro, L. (2019). The functional role of dreaming in emotional processes. *Frontiers of Psychology*, *10*, 459. https://doi.org/10.3389/fpsyg.2019.00459

Schacter, D. L. (2012). Constructive memory: Past and future. *Dialogues in Clinical Neuroscience*, *14*(1), 7–18. https://doi.org/10.31887/DCNS.2012.14.1/dschacter

Schacter, D. L., & Addis, D. R. (2007). The cognitive neuroscience of constructive memory: Remembering the past and imagining the future. *Philosophical Transactions of the Royal Society of London: Series B. Biological Sciences*, *362*(1481), 773–786. https://doi.org/10.1098/rstb.2007.2087

Schacter, D. L., Addis, D. R., Hassabis, D., Martin, V. C., Spreng, R. N., & Szpunar, K. K. (2012). The future of memory: Remembering, imagining, and the brain. *Neuron*, *76*(4), R677–R694. https://doi.org/10.1016/j.neuron.2012.11.001

Schacter, D. L., Chiu, C.-Y. P., & Ochsner, K. N. (1993). Implicit memory: A selective review. *Annual Review of Neuroscience*, *16*, 159–182. https://doi.org/10.1146/annurev.ne.16.030193.001111

Schore, A. (2012). *The science of the art of psychotherapy*. W. W. Norton.

Schultze-Florey, C. R., Martínez-Maza, O., Magpantay, L., Breen, E. C., Irwin, M. R., Gündel, H., & O'Connor, M. F. (2012). When grief makes you sick: Bereavement induced systemic inflammation is a question of genotype. *Brain, Behavior, and Immunity*, *26*(7), 1066–1071. https://doi.org/10.1016/j.bbi.2012.06.009

Schwartz, B. L., & Krantz, J. H. (2016). *Sensation and perception*. Sage.

Scott, K. (2005). Taste recognition: Food for thought. *Neuron*, *48*(3), 455–464. https://doi.org/10.1016/j.neuron.2005.10.015

Seery, M. D. (2011). Resilience: A silver lining to experiencing adverse life events? *Current Directions in Psychological Science*, *20*(6), 390–394. https://doi.org/10.1177/0963721411424740

Seligman, M. E., & Csikszentmihalyi, M. (2000). Positive psychology: An introduction. *American Psychologist*, *55*(1), 5–14. https://doi.org/10.1037//0003-066x.55.1.5

Shakespeare, W. (2003). *Macbeth* (B. A. Mowat & P. Werstine [Eds.]). Simon & Schuster. (Original work published 1623)

Shakespeare, W. (2008). *Sonnet 30* (A. Mabillard, Ed.). (Original work published 1609). http://www.shakespeare-online.com/sonnets/30detail.html

Shear, K., Monk, T., Houck, P., Melhem, N., Frank, E., Reynolds, C., & Sillowash, R. (2007). An attachment-based model of complicated grief including the role of avoidance. *European Archives of Psychiatry and Clinical Neuroscience, 257*(8), 453–461. https://doi.org/10.1007/s00406-007-0745-z

Shuchter, S. R., & Zisook, S. (1993). The course of normal grief. In M. S. Stroebe, W. Stroebe, & R. O. Hansson (Eds.), *Handbook of bereavement* (pp. 23–43). Cambridge University Press. https://doi.org/10.1017/CBO9780511664076.003

Siegel, D. J. (2001). Memory: An overview, with emphasis on developmental, interpersonal, and neurobiological aspects. *Journal of the American Academy of Child and Adolescent Psychiatry, 40*(9), 997–1011. https://doi.org/10.1097/00004583-200109000-00008

Siegel, D. J. (2010). *Mindsight: The new science of personal transformation.* Random House.

Simon, G., VonKorff, M., Piccinelli, M., Fullerton, C., & Ormel, J. (1999). An international study of the relation between somatic symptoms and depression. *The New England Journal of Medicine, 341*, 1329–1334. https://doi.org/10.1056/NEJM199910283411801

Singer, J. A. (2004). Narrative identity and meaning making across the adult lifespan: An introduction. *Journal of Personality, 72*(3), 437–460. https://doi.org/10.1111/j.0022-3506.2004.00268.x

Singer, J. A. (2019). Repetition is the scent of the hunt: A clinician's application of narrative identity to a longitudinal life study. *Qualitative Psychology, 6*(2), 194–205. https://doi.org/10.1037/qup0000149

Singer, J. A., & Blagov, P. (2004). The integrative function of narrative processing: Autobiographical memory, self-defining memories, and the life story of identity. In D. R. Beike, J. M. Lampinen, & D. A. Behrend (Eds.), *The self and memory* (pp. 117–138). Psychology Press.

Smith, G. (2020). *Purposeful breathing.* Exisle.

Smith, J. (2018). Participants and researchers searching for meaning: Conceptual developments for interpretative phenomenological analysis. *Qualitative Research in Psychology, 16*(2), 166–181. https://doi.org/10.1080/14780887.2018.1540648

Smith, K. V., & Ehlers, A. (2021). Prolonged grief and posttraumatic stress disorder following the loss of a significant other: An investigation of cognitive and behavioural differences. *PLOS ONE, 16*(4), e0248852. https://doi.org/10.1371/journal.pone.0248852

Smith, K. V., Wild, J., & Ehlers, A. (2020). The masking of mourning: Social disconnection after bereavement and its role in psychological distress. *Clinical Psychological Science, 8*(3), 464–476. https://doi.org/10.1177/2167702620902748

Snyder, C. R., Harris, C., Anderson, J. R., Holleran, S. A., Irving, L. M., Sigmon, S. T., Yoshinobu, L., Gibb, J., Langelle, C., & Harney, P. (1991). The will and the ways: Development and validation of an individual-differences measure of hope. *Journal of Personality and Social Psychology, 60*(4), 570–585. https://doi.org/10.1037/0022-3514.60.4.570

Snyder, C. R., Irving, L., & Anderson, J. R. (1991). Hope and health: Measuring the will and the ways. In C. R. Snyder & D. R. Forsyth (Eds.), *Handbook of social and clinical psychology: The health perspective* (pp. 285–305). Pergamon Press.

Sormanti, M., & August, J. (1997). Parental bereavement: Spiritual connections with deceased children. *American Journal of Orthopsychiatry, 61*, 460–469. https://doi.org/10.1037/h0080247

Southwick, S. M., & Charney, D. S. (2012, October 5). The science of resilience: Implications for the prevention and treatment of depression. *Science, 338*(6103), 79–82. https://doi.org/10.1126/science.1222942

Staresina, B. P., Gray, J. C., & Davachi, L. (2009). Event congruency enhances episodic memory encoding through semantic elaboration and relational binding. *Cerebral Cortex, 19*(5), 1198–1207. https://doi.org/10.1093/cercor/bhn165

Starr, L. R., & Davila, J. (2012). Responding to anxiety with rumination and hopelessness: Mechanism of anxiety–depression symptom co-occurrence? *Cognitive Therapy Research, 36*, 321–337. https://doi.org/10.1007/s10608-011-9363-1

Steffen, E., & Coyle, A. (2010). Can "sense of presence" experiences in bereavement be conceptualised as spiritual phenomena? *Mental Health, Religion & Culture, 13*, 273–291. https://doi.org/10.1080/13674670903357844

Stolorow, R. D. (2011). *Psychoanalytic inquiry: Vol. 35. World, affectivity, trauma: Heidegger and post-Cartesian psychoanalysis.* Routledge.

Strecher, V. J. (2016). *Life on purpose: How living for what matters most changes everything*. Harper.

Stroebe, M., & Schut, H. (2005). To continue or relinquish bonds: A review of consequences for the bereaved. *Death Studies, 29*(6), 477–494. https://doi.org/10.1080/07481180590962659

Stroebe, M., Schut, H., & Stroebe, W. (2007). Health outcomes of bereavement. *The Lancet, 370*(9603), 1960–1973. https://doi.org/10.1016/S0140-6736(07)61816-9

Stroebe, M., & Stroebe, W. (1991). Does "grief work" work? *Journal of Consulting and Clinical Psychology, 59*(3), 479–482. https://doi.org/10.1037/0022-006X.59.3.479

Sun, P., Smith, A. S., Lei, K., Liu, Y., & Wang, Z. (2014). Breaking bonds in male prairie vole: Long-term effects on emotional and social behavior, physiology, and neurochemistry. *Behavioural Brain Research, 265*, 22–31. https://doi.org/10.1016/j.bbr.2014.02.016

Swann, W. B., Jr., & Bosson, J. K. (2010). Self and identity. In S. T. Fiske, D. T. Gilbert, & G. Lindzey (Eds.), *Handbook of social psychology* (pp. 589–628). Wiley. https://doi.org/10.1002/9780470561119.socpsy001016

Tedeschi, R., & Calhoun, L. G. (2012). *Trauma and transformation: Growing in the aftermath of suffering*. Sage.

Thompson, R. J., & Berenbaum, H. (2006). Shame reactions to everyday dilemmas are associated with depressive disorder. *Cognitive Therapy and Research, 30*(4), 415–425. https://doi.org/10.1007/s10608-006-9056-3

Todd, R. M., Cunningham, W. A., Anderson, A. K., & Thompson, E. (2012). Affect-biased attention as emotion regulation. *Trends in Cognitive Science, 16*(7), 365–372. https://doi.org/10.1016/j.tics.2012.06.00

Tomkins, S. S. (1995). Script theory. In E. V. Demos (Ed.), *Exploring affect: The selected writings of Silvan S. Tomkins* (pp. 389–396). Cambridge University Press.

Tomkins, S. S. (2008). *Affect imagery consciousness*. Springer.

Torges, C. M., Stewart, A. J., & Nolen-Hoeksema, S. (2008). Regret resolution, aging, and adapting to loss. *Psychology and Aging, 23*(1), 169–180. https://doi.org/10.1037/0882-7974.23.1.169

Tugade, M. M., & Fredrickson, B. L. (2004). Resilient individuals use positive emotions to bounce back from negative emotional experiences.

Journal of Personality and Social Psychology, 86(2), 320–333. https:// doi.org/10.1037/0022-3514.86.2.320

Tulving, E. (1993). What is episodic memory? *Current Directions in Psychological Science, 2*(3), 67–70. https://doi.org/10.1111/1467-8721. ep10770899

Tulving, E. (2007). Are there 256 kinds of memory? In L. Roediger III & J. Nairne (Eds.), *The foundations of remembering: Essays in honor of Henry L. Roediger, III* (pp. 39–52). Psychology Press.

Vaccaro, A. G., Kaplan, J. T., & Damasio, A. (2020). Bittersweet: The neuroscience of ambivalent affect. *Perspectives on Psychological Science, 15*(5), 1187–1199. https://doi.org/10.1177/1745691620927708

Västfjäll, D., Peters, E., & Bjälkebring, P. (2011). The experience and regulation of regret across the adult life span. In I. Nykliček, A. Vingerhoets, & M. Zeelenberg (Eds.), *Emotion regulation and well-being* (pp. 165–180). Springer Science + Business Media.

Veilleux, J. C., Conrad, M., & Kassel, J. D. (2013). Cue-induced cigarette craving and mixed emotions: A role for positive affect in the craving process. *Addictive Behaviors, 38*(4), 1881–1889. https://doi.org/10.1016/ j.addbeh.2012.12.006

Vitlic, A., Khanfer, R., Lord, J. M., Carroll, D., & Phillips, A. C. (2014). Bereavement reduces neutrophil oxidative burst only in older adults: Role of the HPA axis and immunesenescence. *Immunity & Ageing, 11*, 13. https://doi.org/10.1186/1742-4933-11-13

Wamsley, E. J., & Stickgold, R. (2011). Memory, sleep and dreaming: Experiencing consolidation. *Sleep Medicine Clinics, 6*(1), P97–P108. https://doi.org/10.1016/j.jsmc.2010.12.008

Wang, Z., Hulihan, T. J., & Insel, T. R. (1997). Sexual and social experience is associated with different patterns of behavior and neural activation in male prairie voles. *Brain Research, 767*(2), 321–332. https://doi.org/ 10.1016/s0006-8993(97)00617-3

Weiss, J. (1993). *How psychotherapy works*. Guilford Press.

Wheeler, M. A., Stuss, D. T., & Tulving, E. (1997). Toward a theory of episodic memory: The frontal lobes and autonoetic consciousness. *Psychological Bulletin, 121*(3), 331–354. https://doi.org/10.1037/0033-2909.121.3.331

Whyte, D. (2015). *The three marriages: Reimagining work, self, and relationship*. Riverhead Books.

Wilson, A. E., & Ross, M. (2003). The identity function of autobiographical memory: Time is on our side. *Memory, 11*(2), 137–149. https://doi.org/10.1080/741938210

Woike, B., & Matic, D. (2004). Cognitive complexity in response to traumatic experiences. *Journal of Personality, 72*(3), 633–657. https://doi.org/10.1111/j.0022-3506.2004.00275.x

Wolfenstein, M. (1966). How is mourning possible? *The Psychoanalytic Study of the Child, 21*, 93–123.

World Health Organization. (2022). *International statistical classification of diseases and related health problems* (11th revision). https://www.who.int/standards/classifications/classification-of-diseases

Wu, G., Feder, A., Cohen, H., Kim, J. J., Calderon, S., Charney, D. S., & Mathé, A. A. (2013). Understanding resilience. *Frontiers in Behavioral Neuroscience, 7*, 10. https://doi.org/10.3389/fnbeh.2013.00010

Wurmser, L. (2015). Primary shame, mortal wound and tragic circularity: Some new reflections on shame and shame conflicts. *International Journal of Psychoanalysis, 96*, 1615–1634.

Zautra, A. J., Affleck, G. G., Tennen, H., Reich, J. W., & Davis, M. C. (2005). Dynamic approaches to emotions and stress in everyday life: Bolger and Zuckerman reloaded with positive as well as negative affects. *Journal of Personality, 73*(6), 1511–1538. https://doi.org/10.1111/j.0022-3506.2005.00357.x

Zeelenberg, M., van Dijk, W. W., van der Pligt, J., Manstead, A. S. R., van Empelen, P., & Reinderman, D. (1998). Emotional reactions to the outcomes of decisions: The role of counterfactual thought in the experience of regret and disappointment. *Organizational Behavior and Human Decision Processes, 75*(2), 117–141. https://doi.org/10.1006/obhd.1998.2784

Zhao, H., Li, D., & Li, X. (2018). Relationship between dreaming and memory reconsolidation. *Brain Science Advances, 4*(2), 118–130. https://doi.org/10.26599/BSA.2018.9050005

INDEX

defined, 182
and future experiences, 19
hope in, 164, 172
impact of emotions on, 59–60
impact of narrative stories on, 152
loss of a child and, 26–29
Erikson, Erik H., 42–43
Excitement, 63, 159
Exercise, 136, 138
Experiences
constructive memory to predict
future, 33
creepy, after loss of loved one, 170
emotional, 65–67
impact of episodic memory on
future, 19
in memories, 21
new, sensory memory and, 125
positive, 159
prevalent positivity and optimism
bias on, 173n1
repetitive sensory, 128–129
shared, 151
Explicit memory
about, 15
and closure, 23
defined, 182
impact of traumatic events on, 24
involuntary, 128
sensory experiences in, 121
sound as trigger for, 131–132

Facial expressions, 63, 65
Factual recollections, 29–37
Failure, 115
False memories, 61
Family members
emotional resonance in relationships
with, 150
as social support, 138
Fear, 63, 162
Fear–terror (affect), 63
Flashbulb memory, 23–24, 182

Flexibility
cognitive, 135–136
resilience and, 163
Food, grief response to, 130
Food cravings, 126–127
Forgetfulness, 100
Fragmented recall, 24
Freud, Sigmund, 22, 27
Freud, Sophie, 27–28
Friendships
bonds of attachment in, 46
emotional resonance in, 150
talking about grief in, 156–157
Future experiences
constructive memory to predict, 33
impact of episodic memory on, 19
prevalent positivity and optimism
bias on, 173n1

Gait, bowed, 135
Gastrointestinal problems, 135
"Goodbye," saying, 26
Grief, 3–9
acceptance and closure in, 7–8
collective, 8
complicated, 50, 53, 181
emotional memories and experience
of, 59–62
as emotional state, 64
emotions in states of, 58–59
Freud on, 27–28
memories and, 5–6
narratives and autobiographical
content in, 8–9
personal and silent, 6–7
prolonged, 49–53, 68, 183
role of shame in, 68–72
stages of, 47
types of, 8
Grief dreams, 30
Grief-related emotional experiences,
65–67
Grief-related memories, 3–6, 8

ABOUT THE AUTHOR

Mary Lamia, PhD, is familiar with loss—she lost her mother in childhood, her father in young adulthood, and her husband of 44 years as she was completing the manuscript for this book. Her own journey underscores her conviction that the people we have lost maintain a presence within the memories that are activated throughout our lives, and that these memories can script who we become. Through her practice as a clinical psychologist in Marin County, California, and her work as a professor at the Wright Institute in Berkeley, California, she endeavors to convey an understanding of emotion. Dr. Lamia is also dedicated to educating the public about the psychology of human behavior, which she achieves by blogging for *Psychology Today*, *Thrive Global*, and *Psychwire*, and providing numerous media interviews and commentaries. With this goal in mind, Dr. Lamia has authored six books, including *Grief Isn't Something to Get Over: Finding a Home for Memories and Emotions After Losing a Loved One*; *Emotions! Making Sense of Your Feelings*; *What Motivates Getting Things Done: Procrastination, Emotions, and Success*; *The Upside of Shame: Therapeutic Interventions Using the Positive Aspects of a "Negative" Emotion*; *Understanding Myself: A Kid's Guide to Intense Emotions and Strong Feelings*; and *The White Knight Syndrome: Rescuing Yourself From Your Need to Rescue Others*.